Amanda De Warren

My Journey

Behind

Blue Eyes

EDITED BY

Vicki Englund

Published by Amanda De Warren 2015

A catalogue record for this book is available from the National Library of Australia.

Edited by Vicki Englund
www.vickienglund.com.au

Cover photograph by Simon Heading

Book cover design and formatting services by BookCoverCafe.com

I'd like to give a big thank you to my good friend, Darren, for all the time and effort you've put in to my beautiful back cover drawing. — Amanda

www.AmandaDeWarren.com

First Edition 2015

ISBN: 978-0-9942471-0-0

TABLE OF CONTENTS

INTRODUCTION
Why I had to write this book

I have often been asked over the years to write my story. I've wanted to write it for such a long time and have had so many ideas for several books, but sometimes it's difficult to know where to start. I guess the best place to start is the beginning… so here it is for you to enjoy. This book shares with you the fascinating journey that I've been on so far and the events that have made me the person I am today.

In this book I wanted to share my journey with you from my early years to how I got to where I am today – a psychic, medium and animal communicator with thousands of loyal clients and fans. People and Spirit have been pushing me for years to get this book up and running, but first I needed to experience many parts of my life to understand how I got to be in the truly blessed position that I am.

I know that there are many sceptics out there and those who think that people who do what I do for a living are frauds. That's okay, they're entitled to their opinion, but anyone who knows me will know that I'm a very genuine person who's always known from early childhood that there was something very different about me. I didn't choose to do what I do – it chose me. But let me assure you that I absolutely love my career and all that it brings to me.

When I was a young child, I had the feeling that I was going to be known around the world for something. I guess you could call it a 'knowing' even though I wasn't sure what that knowing truly was. There was one thing I knew for sure though – from a very young age I was definitely a little different! I knew I could telepathically connect (even though I obviously didn't know or understand that term) to loved ones who had passed and to animals. I could sense things around me and around animals and I thought at the time that this was normal.

I feel my book will help so many others on a similar journey as myself to discover who they really are. Even if you don't think you have psychic abilities, you might find after reading my book that you've had a psychic experience or want to explore the possibility of opening yourself up to that more. This book shares everything about where I've come from to where I am in my journey at this point of writing my book. I trust that it will not only help you get to know me but might help you get to know yourself better and open yourself up to things you might never have thought possible.

I could not have written this without the support and help of others who encouraged me all the way. I have been blessed with two very special parents – Jackie (who passed in 2003) and Eddie. Mum was a nurse and an accomplished horsewoman who taught Mia Farrow to ride in England, while Dad was a draftsman. He'd studied at night school while working on a dairy farm because he was too young for active duty in WWII. He later went on to be a senior prisoner officer for the criminally insane. They both encouraged me from a very young age to always be the person I wanted to be and to embrace the triumphs, losses, and ups and downs in my life which I will also share with you in this book.

Just as I was completing this first book, my father passed away aged 88. I was so blessed to have an amazing dad whom I had a very close bond with, and I loved him with all my heart. I was with him when he passed, and as I stroked his head and held his hand I went through some of the memories we made together and I knew my mother was there waiting to pick him up. Thank you, Dad, for being the remarkable man and father that you will always be to me, and I feel so truly blessed that I had you in my life for as long as I did. Your family all love you and many tears have been shed by them all since you left to be with Mum.

Edward Charles Reading (Ted), 10/08/26 to 14/10/14

I hope that you all enjoy reading this book as much as I've enjoyed writing it.

Love,
Amanda

BIOGRAPHY

*B*efore I go back to the beginning and tell you about my life, I want to share with you my first amazing psychic experience that I can recall quite clearly. I was only a small child in England at the time but this experience is still very clear to me today all these years later.

I was walking across the railway tracks behind my grandparents' garden where I used to spend hours and hours with Granddad in this amazing veggie garden he had. (I really loved him and every time I smell tomatoes I think of him.) I was waiting for my mum to pick me up and she was late. I remember I'd walked over this really old bridge heading towards Junction Road where my grandparents lived. I saw what I felt was a person but not a solid person and I thought, *That looks like Mr. Goss…* but I was sure he'd passed (he'd been my grandparents' neighbour for 40 years). I said, 'Hello Mr. Goss, how are you?' He said, 'My cat's just died.' I knew his fluffy cat and I said, 'Oh my gosh, that's so sad.' He then told me that she'd been run over and that she was now with him. I was only young and said, 'Okay then, see you later.'

I then saw my mum coming towards me in the distance and when she got to me, she said, 'Sorry I'm late.' Mum then asked, 'Who were you talking to?' I said, 'Mr. Goss. He said that his cat had been killed by a car.' Blood drained from Mum's face and she said, 'I'm late because I've just been picking up Mr. Goss's cat off the road and burying it and Mr. Goss has been dead for a couple of years.' My mother had been on her way to pick me up from school but saw the cat on the road. It had still been living up until then with Mr. Goss's daughter. So this man, who'd passed over, told me that his cat had just been killed by a car. Understandably, my mother was very shocked!

You can see that this wasn't the kind of experience most young children have, but I wasn't afraid and didn't think it strange. It was just part of who I was. And now to my story…

WHERE IT ALL STARTED

I was born on 21 July, 1962, a home birth in Potters Lane, Burgess Hill, Sussex, England at two in the afternoon. My father, Edward, sister, Marilyn and brother, Terry were sitting on the internal staircase waiting for my arrival. My mum was a nurse at the time and there was a midwife there. There were no complications and everything went well.

My grandparents, Mary and Walter (my mother's parents), lived five minutes around the corner, while my father's parents had already passed… so I didn't get to connect with them until later on in life! My grandmother, Mary, and grandfather, Walter, passed when I was three and nine respectively – I was extremely close to my grandfather, who's been very influential as a Spirit Guide through my learnings.

Amanda in high chair at 10 months

Unfortunately I didn't get to meet my mother's two sisters who passed before I was born – Aunty Dorothy from a brain haemorrhage at 41, and two years later Aunty Sylvia from a hole in the heart. Aunty Dorothy's death happened in a fish and chip shop across the road from her home. She had three children (one of her daughters has now passed from cancer) and was married to my favourite uncle, Uncle Jim. Sylvia passed suddenly at her farm at the age of 42 – she had five children, and two have also now passed from cancer.

As you might've noticed, cancer has been common in our family – something that was confirmed to me when I connected with Aunty Dorothy when my mother was passing ten years ago. She said that cancer had been hereditary in our family on my grandmother Mary's side.

Other people in my family who have been dear to me are my Dad's sister, Aunty May (whose first husband was killed in WWII and then she remarried a lovely man called Alf), and my dad's brother, Uncle Bill and his wife Lily, whom I got to meet when they came out from England to visit. They have now all passed.

OFF TO AUSTRALIA

For the first two years of my life in England, things were pretty normal. My father, being an engineer, was then offered a fantastic job in Australia at Dalby and Mum contacted the Dalby Hospital and was told she'd definitely have a job there – she was an enrolled nurse. Back then in 1964 you had to have a sponsor to come into the country, and we were lucky enough to have my grandmother Mary's brother, Charlie, living in Toowoomba. 'Uncle Char', who was my mum's favourite uncle, sponsored us. It was a hard decision for Mum to leave England because both her sisters had passed, and Nanny and Granddad only had Mum left, but it was a huge opportunity for my parents to start a new life. We packed up, sold everything and made the big shift from Burgess Hill, Sussex, to Dalby in Queensland. I was two years of age.

Amanda in pram with doll

After we arrived in Australia, our photo was taken by the Brisbane newspaper, *The Courier Mail*, for a story about immigration – we were some of the so-called '10-pound poms'. Uncle Char organised a Housing Commission house and furniture for us – a lengthy process which took about six months with all the back and forth that had to go on (of course there were no such things as text messages, email and the like back then).

We moved into Alfred Street, Dalby, and bought an old blue Falcon car. My sister, Marilyn, was 12 at the time and my brother, Terry, 14. I was only two so can barely remember but it must've been a huge change for my parents and siblings. I've kept a lot of photos and thank goodness I did. Mum and Dad settled into their new jobs easily and Terry and Marilyn made friends at Dalby High School. Thinking back, it would've been a really hard adjustment but it was a good decision that my parents made, and fortunately they had always had a very solid relationship.

Because Dalby was such a small town, Mum would walk to work and pick me up from kindy. The first recollection I have of living in a very hot climate was when Mum would get me an Eskimo Pie ice-cream and we'd go to the park after kindy and play on the swings. Mum would then do her shopping which I think was at a BCC store.

My first real recollection of animals playing a part in my life happened back then. I remember Dad coming home one day after work – I always got excited when he came home as we've always been close – and I looked in the old blue Falcon and there was a dog sitting in the back of it. I was so excited! I said to Mum, 'Dad's got a dog!' and she said, 'Don't be ridiculous,' but I said, 'No, there's a dog there.'

That became our first family pet and her name was Scruffy. She'd wandered into Dad's work at the smelter and the workers had been feeding her. He'd decided that if no-one wanted her, he'd take her home. She was probably about two or three and oh, how I loved her!

By the time I was four, Mum and Dad felt they'd had enough of Dalby and wanted to move to Brisbane. My sister had also decided she wanted to go to university to become a teacher so Mum and Dad made the decision to make a move to Brisbane. We packed up the house and bought a place in Illidge Street, Camp Hill. Of course, Scruffy came with us but she was a car chaser and sadly passed after being hit by a car a few years later.

Three years – at Alfred Street, Dalby

Mum got a job at Mount Olivet Hospital at Kangaroo Point (now known as St. Vincent's Private Hospital), and Dad was offered a new career as a psychiatric nurse for the criminally insane at Wolston Park Hospital in Wacol so he decided to take that. We settled in very well in our new home in Brisbane and I made friends with all the local wildlife. After I finished kindy I started going to Whites Hill State College for the first few months of grade one and then changed to Coorparoo State School, Marilyn began her teaching studies at Mt. Gravatt Teachers'

College, and Terry went into banking. Marilyn had been dating a soldier called Les whom she'd met at 14 in Dalby, a lovely guy who'd been to Vietnam. They stayed together for quite some time and I remember a going-away party for him and his army buddies. He helped Mum and Dad renovate the Illidge Street house.

Seven years – with Scruffy

Mum had always loved horses and really missed them, so she decided she wanted to get another horse. She bought an older horse called Bella from a riding school and we'd ended up with a cat by then too – a stray called Minnie (Minnie Puss), and not long after we got her she had kittens in my sister's bedroom. She had five and we managed to find good homes for four of them. We ended up with Minnie Puss and Big Puss.

I have to mention my very close friend, Heather, whom I met when we lived in Illidge Street. Her older sister, Beverley Anne, was an accomplished dancer who taught us to dance, and her parents owned the local corner shop. We were similar in age and her parents, Bill and Alma, became long-lasting friends of our family. I have this vivid memory of Heather and me, at the grand age of four, deciding one day that we didn't want to go to kindy so we took some lollies and proceeded to head back to my place for the day… until Bill caught up with us up the road and boy, were we in trouble! Heather and her family are still very close to my family even though sadly, we lost the Amazing Alma, as we called her, in 2011.

CHANGE OF PLANS

Mum and Dad were thinking of moving again so we could have horses and other animals, when my grandmother became very sick. Mum and I had to quickly head back over to England while Dad held the fort back in Australia with my siblings. By then, my sister had met her soon-to-be first husband, Seb. He was a law student who was teaching my brother French for the banking industry and he'd come to the Illidge Street house and took an absolute liking to Marilyn, who was second year uni at that stage.

Amanda and Heather – about 7 years – with Minnie Puss and pet dog, Bikkie

Amanda and Heather 45 years later

A couple of our regular routines were that Dad would drop me off and pick me up at Girls Brigade on a Friday night, and we'd always have fish and chips on a Sunday night and watch *Doctor Who* on TV afterwards. Marilyn got a part-time job at a corner store to earn a bit of money and Dad and I would pick her up on Sunday evenings. She would always have a bag of lollies for all of us. By then she'd decided she was going to marry Seb, and we still love him dearly to this day even though they're no longer together.

Now back to Mum and me – my grandmother was dying and when Mum and I flew over to be with her, we arrived very late that night. There were no trains or planes from Heathrow to Burgess Hill back then so we had to catch a taxi. It was well over an hour's drive and it cost about six pounds – a huge amount at the time. We arrived at about one o'clock in the morning and my mother was devastated because my grandmother had passed an hour before we got there. Nan had passed at home and was in the front room because in those days you kept the body in the casket until the funeral. My grandfather was an absolute mess – they'd loved each other dearly for over 50 years.

We ended up staying in England for six months because something terrible happened while we were sorting everything out – my grandfather died about four months after we got there. I knew this was going to happen – I experienced that first feeling of impending loss which was going to become something common in my life in later years. Mum found Granddad in his bed – he had passed in his sleep, and I knew he was with Nan once again. We had to sell the home that Mum had grown up in, and this was really hard for her as she'd lost both her parents and her sisters, and Mum was the only one left.

MY FIRST PSYCHIC EXPERIENCES

While we were over in England, Mum got a job working as a nurse in a home for Down Syndrome children and I would go to meet her there after school. I loved these people – I'd sit down and play games with them and would talk to them. Somehow I just connected with them. And I always felt and knew things through them.

From a young age – about three or four – I could sense people who were passed over around me. When Nan's body was in the coffin in the front room, I knew she was there and I would talk to her and also to my two passed-over aunties. I would say to Mum, 'Aunty Dorothy is always eating caramel toffee. Why is she always eating it?' Mum would say, 'How did you know that? That was her favourite,' and I'd say, 'She tells me.'

It was around about the time when I was attending Burgess Hill School in England that I had the first psychic connection I can totally recall and which I detailed at the beginning of this book about Mr. Goss and his cat. After that, the psychic experiences continued to come regularly.

My mum worked just around the corner, and if she was working late I'd be picked up by Mrs. Franklin, a lovely elderly friend of my grandparents. I can still see her face. I was in Mrs. Franklin's front room one day and I felt this man sitting there. He was in a blue military looking uniform and sitting in this great big chair, smoking a pipe and looking at me. This big fluffy cat was also sitting beside him on the armchair. The man said, 'My name is Bert. I'm Mrs. Franklin's husband. I had a heart attack right in this chair and I died.' I thought it was kind of creepy but I never got scared.

Amanda and her mother, Jackie, in Egypt en-route to England

I said to Mrs. Franklin, 'There's a man called Bert here. He's sitting in that chair.' She obviously couldn't see him and I said, 'Can't you see him?' Her eyes were like saucepans and she said, 'No. Go on.' And I said, 'Robert tells me that he died of a sudden heart attack in that chair. I'm smelling smoke and he's smoking a pipe. He's wearing a blue military uniform.' Tears welled up in her eyes and she exclaimed, 'Oh my God!' And I said, 'There's more. There's a big fluffy cat sitting on the armchair right beside him.' Mrs. Franklin just completely lost it and was crying as she said, 'Darling, you are going to be famous, I know you are. You've just described my husband Bert, a military man. He bought me that cat; his name was Tudor.' She also told me that Bert had died of a heart attack in that chair and the cat had never left that chair after he passed. The cat also passed in the chair! Of course I hadn't possibly known any of this as I'd never heard them mentioned before.

As a child, I often stayed at my Uncle Norman's farm, called Redhouse Farm, in Mayfield, Sussex. He had been married to my Aunty Sylvia (he's still a farmer and is 91 at the time of writing this). It was a dairy farm – cows, sheep, dogs, cats, horses, everything. It was just wonderful and I'd spend weekend after weekend there, beginning to communicate with the animals and saying some very strange stuff which I thought was normal. 'Can't you hear what they're saying?' I'd say, shocked that no-one else could hear the animals' thoughts.

One day, we were on the tractor and one of the farm dogs went missing. I felt the dog had fallen down off a big haystack and I said to my two cousins, Cherry (now deceased) and Robyn, 'The dog's fallen down the back of the haystack and it's right down the end of the farm. He's jumped up and fallen and he's wedged between the haystack and the shed.' Naturally, everyone was wary but I was so insistent that we took the tractor which the farm hand, Gordon, drove. When I pointed out which haystack the dog was behind, we got there and could hear the dog barking. Gordon got up on this huge haystack, looked down, and lo and behold, he saw the dog! It was crying and calling out and of course everyone was really shocked.

7 years – professional photo of her holding book

So everything really started to happen from then. I had had the odd inkling of things at about four to five years of age but they were my first real memories of being a medium and an animal communicator.

BACK TO AUSTRALIA

Mum and I came back to Australia as my sister, Marilyn, was getting married to Seb, who'd finished his solicitor's degree by then. We'd kept Mum's Palomino horse, Bella, at a friend's house, and Dad and Mum had decided they wanted somewhere closer to where the horses were. Dad had bought another house in Mt. Gravatt while Mum and I were in England, so when we returned we lived in the Mt. Gravatt house and I started in about grade three at Upper Mt. Gravatt State School. Even though my schooling had been very interrupted by this stage, I settled in quite well. It was a great location too as we were only 15 minutes from the horse and it was near the teaching college. Marilyn and Seb had bought their first house, a nice old place in South Brisbane, and she was finishing her teaching degree.

Amanda with Snippy after winning dressage

Amanda and Rory at Pallara

Minnie Puss and Big Puss were still alive at this stage but sadly not long after that, Big Puss was killed by a dog. Mum and I had to go back to England once again to sort the house out over there, but that time it was only for about a month.

Life went on as it does, and after a few years I was doing okay at MacGregor High School where I loved art, geography, history and music. I wasn't too bad at sport either, being in the softball team at primary and high school, and I was in the netball team as well. I remember in grade seven that we got into the softball semi-finals for the whole of Brisbane. We played against Aspley and lost but we got to go and watch the finals. I went on to play softball for quite awhile after that.

After Mum sold the England house, she decided she wanted a property for the horses. I was in pony club by that stage with my horse called Snip – Little Snippy was a bad tempered little bugger! Because the horses weren't living with us, Mum and I had to go to the property to tend to them every afternoon, and Mum got fed up with that so she and Dad bought ten acres of land for the horses just off Teviot Road in Greenbank. Snip and I won the South East Queensland dressage when I was 12 but then I outgrew and sold him, and Mum sent me to a summer camp where I fell in love with a horse called Rory. He was a riding school horse but Mum convinced them to sell him to us, however we had to leave him up in Gympie until we'd moved.

That was the decisive moment that Mum said we were moving. We sold the house at Upper Mt. Gravatt and the Greenbank land and moved to Pallara just outside Acacia Ridge (which meant a change of school for me – to Salisbury High School), where we bought a two-storey brick house with five acres of land. It was an older style house and we were able to have all the horses there, which was wonderful. Mum had a horse called Prince and her other horse Bella had a foal called Tiffany before eventually passing away from old age. We buried Bella at Pallara.

FIRST LOVES

I went to pony club at Runcorn for quite some time but quit after we moved to Pallara as it was too far to go. While attending Salisbury High School, I made some lifelong friends, some of whom I'm still very close to – Lisa, Debbie, Sonia and Tanya. I also started to notice boys!

Lisa, Debbie, Amanda, Tanya and Sonia at dinner in 2014

I had settled into life at Pallara, Mum and Dad renovated the house, and we had the horses with us so all was good. When I was about 15, I had long blonde hair, blue eyes and was quite skinny and had been asked to do a little bit of modelling. I'd been in a couple of magazines but didn't really like it much so I'd decided it wasn't for me. I wanted to stay at school where I was doing quite well and get an education.

One day around this time, I was out riding and this guy in a Ford Escort panel van drove past and wolf whistled at me. He did a U turn and came up with all his mates in the back of the panel van and said, 'Geez, you're gorgeous. What's your name?' I thought, *You're pretty interesting*, and I said, 'I'm Mandy.' He said, 'I'm Ian. What are you doing tonight? Where do you live?' I'd been out with a couple of boys before but nothing major.

So Ian, who was 17, came around that night and we started going out. We'd been together for a few months when he came over and picked me and my friend Suzie up to go to a football match to see his best mate, Steve, playing. We were coming around a corner and a van lost control in the wet and hit us head on. Our panel van rolled and the impact was so hard that the steering wheel ended up pushed up against the roof. Luckily, none of us were killed. Sue and Steve were in the back of the van – back then seatbelts weren't compulsory and we didn't have any – and we were all injured. The most frightening sight of my life was seeing this big van coming towards us and not being able to do anything.

The ambulance came and I was in and out of consciousness. I'd bitten right through my tongue and had severe whiplash, lacerations across my face and down my body, and I was black and blue down my left hand side from bruising. Mum and Dad got to the hospital just as the ambulance pulled up with me in it. Ian went to hospital but was released, whereas I stayed in hospital for five days and still have some very fine scars on the left side of my chin. I also can't feel the right hand side of my tongue.

That accident brought about the end of the relationship between me and Ian. He lived at Jindalee and I was at Pallara so even though we stayed in contact by phone, it kind of fizzled out because he didn't have a car anymore. I still liked him – he was my first love – but because we couldn't see each other, he started seeing someone else. But of course things aren't always straightforward and he was in and out of my life.

The next guy to come into my life was Ross. One day I went to the EKKA (the annual Brisbane show or 'Exhibition') with my friend, Donna, and she had met this guy called Greg who worked on the Dodgem Cars. He was six foot two, a wild surfie with hair everywhere, and he got his mate Ross to bring him over to see Donna at my house. Ross had very curly hair, he was drop dead gorgeous, and we just hit it off straight away. Meanwhile, Ian had got a new Holden HQ panel van and was still hovering around but we were no longer together. I had started seeing Ross, so it was kind of a Ross-Ian, Ian-Ross thing for about two years. I would see Ian and finish it with him and then see Ross and finish it with him!

As you might've noticed, I have an interest in different makes and models of cars. When it came time to buy my own first car, it was a Holden GTS Torana. I'd finished school and wasn't sure what I wanted to do, and got my first job at Tip Top Bread as a receptionist and stayed there for quite awhile. I sold the Torana to a friend and bought a white Holden Monaro with a blue stripe up the middle! I moved out of home with a girlfriend of mine and it had basically fizzled out completely between Ian and me, but we were still friends. I was still friends with Ross too but he had a new girlfriend by then and I think she got a bit dirty about it after awhile.

I'll add here that Ross and I are still friends to this day, and funnily enough he works at Australia Zoo, which is a nice connection seeing as I used to work with the Irwins at the Queensland Reptile and Fauna Park – more about that later.

Ross is a lovely guy, a very gentle man, and of course he loves animals.

DARK PREMONITIONS

During this time, I'd still been telepathically communicating with the horses and other people's animals. One day when I was about 17, there was this whole group of friends indulging in drugs and alcohol. I never drank and wasn't into drugs – I'd smoked a bit of pot but I didn't like it so had decided that drugs and alcohol were not for me. I'd moved into a unit with my friend, Suzie, and I was working at another job by then at an engineering company and contemplating doing studies.

I was driving home one day and went to my friend, Shirley's place at Acacia Ridge. (I'd made friends with her at school.) I just got this horrible gut feeling that something wasn't right, and when I waved good-bye to Shirley I gave her a big hug and said, 'I love you forever, you know that. Can you please be careful? I've got a bad feeling.' When I left, I cried in the car and I couldn't work out why. I was just sobbing. It was like the last time I was ever going to see her alive. Two days later, I went to my parents' house and on my way I had to detour because a car had crashed into a pole and both occupants had been killed. As I looked at the fire engines and so forth as I detoured around, I just thought, *Oh my God*. I just had this feeling. About half an hour later at Mum and Dad's, my friend Deb rang me and said, 'Shirley's just been killed in an accident.' Shirley and her boyfriend, Steve, had both been killed in the accident I had just passed. I was just shattered and the first person I rang was Ross. He was really good about it and came over and comforted me.

This was not going to be the last of that sort of premonition concerning close friends, and to this day I still get them. With Shirley, I really felt a sense of loss and the need to warn her and to tell her to be careful. I couldn't pinpoint it but it was just an enormous sadness inside me. The night that it happened, for some reason I just had this strong feeling to go to my parents' place and I'd said to Suzie, 'I've just got to go to Mum and Dad's.'

I remember going to Shirley's funeral, and while everybody else was crying and devastated – and obviously I was too – I felt this enormous sense of peace. I saw an image of her sitting on her coffin and it was just this beautiful, peaceful, quiet image. I remember it so clearly. She was just looking at me and dressed in white – it wasn't exactly a dress but a flowing cover of some kind around her. It's hard to describe and I kept that to myself at the time because I didn't want to upset anyone with something that might've frightened them or made them feel strange towards me.

Another one of my premonitions concerned Carla, a good friend I'd made at MacGregor High School, who was very intelligent but sadly, had got into the drugs. She'd given birth to a little boy about six months earlier and even though I'd moved, I'd stayed in contact with her and she rang me one day to pick her up. I was at Mum and Dad's tending to the horses and I went and got her from East Brisbane – she looked absolutely shocking. She walked down the stairs and she looked so gaunt. She said, 'Can you please take me away from here?' She just wanted to get away from the drugs, so I took her to her parents' house where the baby was. I remember saying to her, 'If you don't do something about it, you're going to die soon.' Again there was the dread, the gut feeling. Not that you needed to be psychic – you could probably tell by looking at her that if she didn't do something soon, this would be the end.

Carla was trying to clean herself up but apparently the baby's father was heavily into drugs. She was very beautiful with long blonde hair and blue eyes, so intelligent and such a beautiful person with so much going for her – I'll never forget it. She said, 'I'm trying to get off the drugs, I'm trying really hard.' But I thought, no. I could sense death, I just knew it. I said, 'I've got death around you, honey, just like I did around Shirley. And I know something is going to go wrong.' She said, 'I know, I've got to get off them but it's so hard.' Three days later I got a phone call. She had overdosed and died. She was 18. Again, I was shattered.

So, I'd lost two close friends, but life goes on and you have no choice but to go on yourself. I ended up meeting a lovely guy called Daryl who came over to my house with some friends from school who I was still close with. I worked out I'd gone to school with his brother, Mark, at Salisbury High School (which closed in 1997). Daryl and I hit it off really well and we formed a close relationship. He had a really flash, hot car too! It was a dark blue, two-door Datsun 240K and he loved this car. Back then it was the bee's knees and you just had to be seen in it.

Daryl and I and his two younger sisters headed to Coffs Harbour to his grandparents' place on the way to Sydney to see his family. As we were driving down, I looked at him and said, 'Daryl, we're going to have an accident.' He said not to be silly but I was a nervous wreck all the way down there. I insisted we were going to have a head-on. Just before we got to Taree, a woman came out from a side street and planted us on the left hand side, smashing the left front of the 240K and my door. She hadn't realised that she was entering the main road and she just crashed straight into us. Luckily, no-one was hurt very badly – I'd told everyone to put their seatbelts on so luckily they had. So that was the demise of the 240K and once again I'd been right with my premonition. I just knew it… and more was to come.

Daryl had this friend called Glen, who was a rough nut but in a really cheeky kind of way. He came over to Daryl's place one day and he'd just bought this new Monaro (I was driving a Mazda Capella Rotary by then) and he had pulled up behind me. I looked in the rear view mirror and I froze. Again, I just saw the dreaded death. I kept looking at this car and thinking, *He's gonna die in that, he's gonna die.* I was getting really upset again. This was probably about nine months to a year after Carla had died so I knew the whole death feeling, especially after Shirley's passing too. I said to Glen, 'You need to be very careful', as again I was feeling the death energy. He said, 'Don't give us that hocus pocus stuff, I'll be alright,' and he laughed.

At a party a week later, as Glen and his girlfriend were leaving I said to her, 'Make sure you tell him you love him.' She said, 'Why?' and I said, 'I've just got this feeling.' I said to Glen again, 'You need to be really, really careful.' As he backed out of the driveway I thought, *Oh my gosh, I'm not going to see him again.* This was on the Saturday night, then on the Monday afternoon he was taking a friend home from work along the Pacific Highway and a woman came from a side street and hit him (similar to the way it had happened with Daryl and me). He spun and rolled, his head hit the concrete and he died instantly. His friend Steve broke his leg.

So there again, the feeling of dread and death had happened just like before. Bear in mind that these were three people within about 14 months that I knew were going to leave this world early. And can you believe it – there's more.

We all used to go to the pub and meet up and dance in a group and about two months after Glen died, I looked at his friend, Steve, and I went, *Oh no*. I just knew that familiar feeling of death. Whenever I looked at him, I would get the feeling of what was going to actually happen. With Glen I felt the accident, I felt the rolling. With Steve I felt choking, like I couldn't breathe. I wondered if it was drowning. A week after I'd seen him at the Salisbury Hotel, he was found dead. He had drunk too much, vomited and choked on it. Again, there had been this feeling of absolute death. I had even said to my friend, Sandra, 'He's going to die of choking.' I might add that just like at Shirley's funeral, I saw Glen, Steve and Carla at their funerals and I felt peace. I can still sense them all around me to this day.

NEW LIVES

As you might expect, some of my friends had started to get spooked by now and I got a bit of a reputation. My friends seemed to be dropping off like flies. Daryl and I went our separate ways by then but we were still friends. I moved over to the other side of town to the suburb of Coorparoo, was working in an electronics warehouse as a receptionist and had bought myself another Monaro – a gold one, sort of in memory of Glen.

While working at the electronics store, I would park my car at the back of a nearby petrol station. This young man of 17, who was an apprentice with the mechanics there, broke into my car to find out where I lived and what my name was! I thought this was quite amusing and my lifelong friendship with the 'Italian stallion' Sam was formed. We have stayed friends through all of our ups and downs through life and he is very special to me.

But I was soon to meet the father of my first child. One day this delivery driver walked in and I thought, *Geez, he's hot!* His name was Paul. We started chatting and it just so happened that every time Paul was due to turn up, I made sure I was in the storeroom for when he dropped his deliveries off. One day he said, 'What's your phone number, hot stuff?' I gave it to him and he said, 'Be home at four o'clock, I'm going to ring you.' So he rang me and came over and that was the start of something.

We moved in together when I was 19 and I'd just turned 20 when I got this awful flu. I was so sick, throwing up and so forth. I must've thrown up my contraceptive pill because next minute I knew I was having a baby. I thought, *Holy crap, I'm pregnant*! I met Paul at work and we went to the doctor and got the positive results. I'd managed to stay 'unpregnant' when 75 per cent of my friends had had babies so I thought I'd been doing quite well!

Paul and I got married at the church my sister had got married at in Coorparoo. It was a very quick wedding! My sister gave me her wedding dress to wear – she'd had three children by then, she was a teacher and they had a beautiful old house in Coorparoo. We settled down in Gordon Park on the north side of Brisbane, and Paul worked while I stayed at home. We had sold the Monaro and bought a little Holden Gemini.

Our daughter, Layla, was born on 15 December, at 4.18am at the Mater Hospital in Brisbane. It was a Friday morning and she was born five weeks early, weighed four pounds eight ounces, and had to stay in a humidicrib for awhile. Paul and I had been living in a flat at Annie Street in Torwood before her birth, and my sister would pick me up and take me to my antenatal hospital visits with her three children. Just after Layla was born when I was still in hospital with her, Paul and Mum and a few other people moved us from the Torwood unit to the house in Gordon Park, which is near Kedron. This was two days before Christmas. We came out of hospital Christmas Eve and spent Christmas Day at my mum's place. We still hadn't unpacked, we had a new baby and a new house, we were trying to settle into life and being married, and we didn't have much money.

During this time, I tried to push my psychic gifts aside but it would still rise every now and then. I would pick up feelings and say things from time to time, but I was caught up in my new life as a wife and mother. As it happened, Paul and I were two different people – he was very much on the wild side and was caught out a few times so we went our separate ways. I was suddenly a single mother studying nursing with a three year-old daughter.

I was finding it hard but I had the support of my family, and Paul was still a very good father.

Layla as baby

By this time I'd bought a new car – a Holden V8 Commodore (yes, I do love my cars!) – but I couldn't afford to run the V8 because I was paying for babysitting while I worked and paying rent for a unit as we had sold our home that we'd bought at Bethania. So it was pretty tough and I had been on my own for quite awhile… but then love raised its head again. I met my son's father, Les, at a car yard when I was looking for a new car – he was the person who looked after the mechanical side of things and he helped me a lot. We started seeing each other and he suggested that instead of me renting a unit with my friends, why didn't we get a place together. So he and I moved in. And guess what he drove? A Monaro. A gold one!

Again, I got sick and the good old pill must've gone down the toilet. Next minute I know, I'm having my son, Luke. It was in the height of summer, stinking hot, and I was in labour. They'd told me it was probably Braxton Hicks contractions because it was too early in the pregnancy, but I knew it wasn't. Luke came into the world screaming, born on Sunday, 24 January, at 7.48pm in the QE2 Hospital. He was seven weeks premature and weighed four pounds two ounces so was even smaller than Layla had been (I'd given birth to them both naturally). So once again, I had an extended hospital stay.

Luke as baby

By now, my parents had had enough of Pallara and, wanting to retire, had bought a house at South MacLean just outside of Jimboomba. Les and I moved out to my parents' property. They still had many animals and I had a little dog called Mindy that was given to me, my fluffy cat, Fleabee, and we ended up with a big fluffy dog called... Fluffy! Paul had moved on and had another daughter, Olivia, with someone else by then. I claim her as my own and she is my 'third child' so to speak. We're close and her two children are my grandchildren as far as I am concerned.

My parents had the two-bedroom granny flat at the new place and Les, Layla, Luke and I had the big house. Luke loved Les's father, Vince, and also spent a lot of time at his property in Tara. Over the years, I still had inclinations and psychic feelings, and one time when we saw Les's grandfather, I knew it was the last time we were going to see him alive. I sensed that feeling of passing and sadly he left this planet about a week later. Even though I knew I had these gifts, I was focusing on raising a family and wanted to be a stay-at-home mother. Les had a good job in the steel industry and we paid cheap rent to my parents who were away a lot travelling all over the world. In return, I looked after the animals for them and made sure everything at the property was okay.

During this time, I met my best friend for the next 23 years, Peter , or 'Daggies' as he was fondly known to me. I called him that because of the character, Dagwood, from the Blondie cartoon strip, because of the hair that stuck out at the sides as Daggies' always did. He was slightly Down Syndrome and we met when Les started working at the steel mill. He invited him over to a barbecue, and although he was very shy at first he started to become a part of our family. When my two kids were growing up he was a part of their lives too – wherever I was, Daggies was not far behind me. When Les and I split, Daggies was always my best friend and very much loved and accepted by all my other friends. We all loved him dearly but he passed from heart complications in 2012 and I still miss him every day. He was cheeky and funny and would always cheer me up with his silly phone calls.

ANIMAL CONNECTIONS

Sadly, Les and I split when Luke was about five. Mum and Dad were selling their property and I was really starting to get into communicating with the animals by then. One day I was coming along the road to my house in MacLean when I saw an injured bearded dragon. I saw that its leg had been hurt and I picked it up and brought it home. I made some phone calls but no-one could help me so I took it upon myself to look after it. Word got around that I'd looked after a bearded dragon and had released it, so I started getting phone calls about it. I found myself being the 'guru' of bearded dragons and I had 18 at one stage, rehabilitating them and releasing them back into the wild.

Daggies – 45 years

Meanwhile, I'd been regularly ringing the Queensland Reptile and Fauna Park to ask for advice. One day Terri Irwin answered the phone and she asked me to come and visit so she could show me around. This was just before her husband Steve Irwin, the famed Crocodile Hunter, had started filming for TV, so he wasn't known yet and his parents, Lyn (who has now passed) and Bob Irwin, were still there. I took my son up there and had a great day, and I stayed in contact with them. I was then offered a job at the park which I accepted.

Amanda with koala at Dreamworld

A few years went by and I was now a single mother of two, studying zoology, and I also now worked three days a week at the Queensland Reptile and Fauna Park.

Les and Luke lived at the Greenbank property bought years earlier, and they ended up putting a demountable home on the land and Mum and Dad lived there too. Because I was working so much and in a rental house at Browns Plains, it was better that Luke stay with Les, and my daughter decided it was easier for her to go and live with her father at Lowood up past Ipswich. Something had to give so I ended up dropping the zoology studies. I remember falling asleep at two o'clock in the morning with my head in the books. I just couldn't do it any longer.

I'd been working with Steve and Terri Irwin for about 18 months (more about that in the Animal Communications chapter), and in that time I'd met someone else who I'll call D. He was very abusive and controlling – he actually threatened my parents and said he'd kill me. It was a very violent relationship which lasted for about four months and thank goodness neither of my children was living with me at the time.

I quickly got out of that relationship and shifted jobs because I was offered a fulltime job at Koala Country at the Gold Coast theme park, Dreamworld. I absolutely loved it! I spent three years there and used to love catching the steam train from Central Station at Dreamworld down to Koala Country. During that time I started to really get to know the train driver, Pete, and about 18 months after I met him I married him! We were organising a wedding, living at his parents' place in a tin shed in the garden and also building a house. The day we moved into the house and were getting the keys, my father had urgent triple bypass surgery – not a good omen! But I knew my father was going to live and he did.

While Peter and I were trying to get the money together to build the house, I was making some extra cash in the evenings with a second job at Dreamworld in the laundry. I formed a special bond and lifelong friendship with the girls in the laundry and we have all remained friends for a very long time.

During that time with Peter and then later while I was at the newly built Jimboomba house, my son Luke became very close to his best friends from school, Chris and Ryan, who are still his best friends today even though they have all grown up and had families of their own. There was always a big group of them at my home and often I'd wake up to a see a sea of kids covering my lounge room after a night of playing the latest video games on the new TV Luke had conned me into buying!

I won't go into too much detail, but sadly Pete and I went our separate ways. It was with great regret but for my own personal emotional state, I felt I had no other choice. He's now remarried with two beautiful children and is still the steam train driver to this day at Dreamworld. We're still very good friends and he will always have a special place in my heart.

While I was still living at the house with Pete, my grown-up children would often visit and stay weekends, and I then got offered a job at Mt. Tamborine Wildlife Sanctuary, which I gladly took. Again, I very much connected with the animals. I just knew what was wrong with them physically and emotionally. I even knew what they wanted to eat. People would ask, 'How do you know that?' or 'Why will that kangaroo come up to you and no-one else?'

I helped run and build up the Mount Tamborine Wildlife Sanctuary along with two lovely ladies – their parents owned the sanctuary at Cedar Creek Falls. We worked hard to bring in animals such as dingos and owls and I always knew what these animals wanted. We refused to put them in small cages – they all had freedom – and if they had to be in cages it was because they weren't releasable and so we could give them the best care. We brought in barking owls and dingos and other species of animals, and worked tirelessly 12-15 hours a day, calling in voluntary help. I would say to the animals, 'Is this what you want? Are you happy here?' and I would get the answer, 'Yes.' The koalas loved their enclosure – they were very happy. They had massive pens and the best of care. We worked hard with very little money, and we built that business up – something of which I'm very proud.

While I was working at the sanctuary, there was a lovely man called Rick who would often help us out after he'd finished work. He actually worked at Thunderbird Park nearby but liked to give a lot of his time to help us girls out. He was only in his mid-forties and a really likable guy. One day, Rick was helping us with an enclosure and once again I had that feeling of dread. I felt an impact and a passing and I felt it was going to happen very soon. Rick lived on the mountain and rode a motorbike to and from work, and on this particular day I said to him, 'Please be careful on that bike.' The next morning we heard that Rick had been hit by a car and killed earlier that morning. I heard the sirens and got this feeling of dread once again. I went to his funeral on the Gold Coast and felt his peaceful presence during the funeral.

Eric – 44 years

THE AMAZING ERIC

Meanwhile, another very special and important man had come into my life – Eric. He was an extremely spiritual man, and when I met him I knew that he didn't have a long time to live.

I again had that feeling of him leaving this planet early. I spent some time with him to get to know him and I just felt this very powerful connection. It wasn't an 'in love' connection; it was a very spiritual connection and we became very close friends. He was never my lover – he was a mentor, a teacher and just a beautiful man to me. It was like I'd known him before and I know that I did in many past lives. When I met him I said, 'Where have you been? I've been waiting for you to come back into my life.'

One day, I knew something was going on with him. He called and asked me to pick him up from work. I just had this feeling of dread around him and I knew that he was going to die. The number 46 came to me and I knew he wouldn't last until 46 – he was 45 at the time. I picked him up after work, looked at him and just thought, *He's going to die, something is wrong.* I felt he had a lung tumor. I took him to the hospital, he had a scan done that same day and there was this massive tumor in the left lung and going right up to his face. They put him in hospital for chemotherapy and radiation treatment, and during those 12 weeks I saw him deteriorate and knew he was going to die. The doctors were saying not to give up hope but once again I just knew.

By now my daughter, Layla, was studying to be a pharmacist and was getting married to Brad, who'd been with her since she was 15, and my son was doing his boilermaking apprenticeship and had bought his first car (an old Holden). I was still working at the animal sanctuary and was in and out of hospital visiting Eric because I was all he had. On this particular day, I knew I had to get up to that hospital and I was rushing to get there. He'd had an operation and I sat with him holding his hand as he said to me, 'I love you the universe.' I held onto his hand and I just knew he was going and he knew too. He said, 'Thank you.' With that, his head just flopped to the side and he passed.

Eric had bought a white cat for company called Purrl Puss and I'd had to go back to the house a lot to look after her when he was in hospital. After Eric passed, I went to the door of his house and I felt this peace and I felt him say to me, 'I love you the universe.' I knew he was connecting to me and that he was at peace. He was saying he was okay and I was going to be okay too. Little did I know at the time that he had changed his superannuation arrangements to benefit me. That was a surprise getting a phone call from the super company saying that half was to go to me and half to his son. I've still got Eric's ashes and I also kept Purrl Puss!

THE SPIRITUAL DOORS OPEN

After Eric passed, the dam doors opened for me spiritually. It was like this amazing… *whoooshka!* I started hearing things, seeing things and smelling things. It was like it was 20 times more powerful than it had ever been before. I looked at Eric's ashes and I said, 'You are responsible for this!' It was a feeling of knowing; I just knew where I was meant to be. And actually, the second Eric passed, I knew it. I got to his house and Purrl was at the door and I just fell to the ground and I cried and cried and cried. I thought to myself that the world had just lost a beautiful man. He was also a very sad man as he'd had a lot of sorrow in his life. When I was crying at his house, I felt that he picked me up off the ground and was saying to me, 'Hey, this is the beginning of a new life for you! It's a spiritual journey for you now, with the animal communication and mediumship. You are going to become someone famous.' I had always known that deep down and it had never gone away but Eric confirmed it for me.

I went back to my home in Jimboomba to start my new life as Peter and I were still living in the same house.

MY SPIRITUAL JOURNEY CONTINUES

I know that what I'm about to tell you might sound completely amazing and maybe even unbelievable in parts, but I can assure you that it's absolutely the truth of what happened to me in the years following Eric's passing. It's what made me who I am today and what gave me the knowledge and skills to use my gift and become a professional medium.

I'll just go back a little to Eric's funeral when Peter and I were still living under the same roof at Jimboomba but living separate lives, as this is where it really began. I remember sitting in the funeral home. I went up to say good-bye to Eric's body and I just felt him around in a very strong, powerful presence. At first I just had this enormous feeling of grief but then all of a sudden it was like the grief was replaced with peace, and I knew he was saying to me, 'Don't grieve. Don't cry for me, I'm not very far away, and I will always be with you.' And he thanked me for being there for him. He told me he had joined his father and his daughter and that he was happy, and that he would help me find someone new in my life.

I knew this was the beginning of something just so massive and so extremely life-changing, and I wanted to do something different so I could concentrate on my spiritual journey. I began to seek out people who I felt could help me discover what I really needed to know, thanks once again to Eric. He had passed in November, 2000, just after the 9/11 terrorist tragedies, and he came through in a connection to me and took me back to that terrible day. I just felt all of these souls call out to me, wanting to connect with me.

Eric said, 'Remember the night that I called you and told you about 9/11?' He brought a man called Christopher through, and a man called Michael, a firefighter, who told me that his brother had survived 9/11 but he had not. Michael also said his father's name. I checked it out in the records of who had been involved that day and who had been killed and indeed that was all true! This was only a few days after Eric's passing when I was feeling very lost, and after that my life started to be consumed with searching. I was determined to find out the truth about the afterlife, even though I felt I already knew the truth in many ways. On a human scale, I needed to know – how did I know this information of someone who had passed on the other side of the world in such tragic circumstances?

ASHKIYA ENTERS MY LIFE

I began to hear, sense, feel, smell and taste, and the awareness personified into many, many strange events. I would wake up at 2am and hear voices chattering and people running up and down the hallway – this was in 2001. I was starting to write a journal and the people told me to go and get a computer. I had a feeling of this lady who I thought was called Ashkira at first, but actually it's Ashkiya, my Ascended Master – a beautiful, seven foot-tall being of pure love. I was made aware of her, I was never afraid of her and I was told that she is an Ascended Master (and I'll tell you more about her in the coming pages). Eric was there too sometimes but he was a completely different soul altogether. He was six foot four and Ashkiya towered above him. I also became aware of my grandfather, Walter, on my mother's side – a very strong presence around guiding me as well. I went out and bought the computer as I'd been told to, and I took some time off from working as I wanted to try and find myself.

I was feeling quite lost and not sure of what I wanted to do next, but then I got a sign. Daggies came over as he normally did every weekend and he knew how sad I was feeling about Eric. That night I had a very powerful dream of Eric and me in Paris. It was a dream I'd never had before and it was so lifelike. We were walking over a small, concrete arched bridge that was very old with old streetlights along the bridge and I was looking at the Arc de Triomphe. Eric took me to a coffee shop and we were sitting having coffee.

When I woke up the next morning, I felt quite bizarre. At this stage, I had been asking for a sign. I said, 'If there is a sign, then I will believe you' (about what I was supposed to be doing with my life). Anyway, the next morning after the dream, Daggies – who loved to travel a lot – pulled out a brochure, put it on the table and said, 'Oh, I forgot to tell you – I'm thinking of going overseas again.' He hadn't even mentioned Paris, but guess what that one brochure was for? Paris! I looked at the Arc de Triomphe and an arched bridge with little lights and the cafés just like I'd seen in my dream and I thought, *Holy crap*! I looked up and said, 'Thank you for the sign.' That was the beginning of my learnings of the spirit world and the Universal University, which I'll tell you more about soon.

Amanda's grandfather, Walter

So many interesting things happened after that. I had this feeling from Eric to go online, and one of my dreams with him in it was that he took me over the Sunshine Coast Motorway – we loved the Sunshine Coast. So we were floating above the motorway holding hands – his soul and my soul – and at the end of it he took a left turn and said, 'I'm going to hand you over to someone else now. You will meet him online and you will move to the Sunshine Coast with him.' And he showed me a blue house.

The dreams continued but I was busy during the day preparing for my daughter Layla's upcoming wedding to Brad in the April after Eric passed, and that occupied a lot of my time. Just as a nice little side note – by then, I had since received Eric's superannuation which I promptly put in the bank after I'd bought a Nissan 300ZX which he always wanted me to have and which I've still got to this day! I don't use it often – it gets put away and is increasing in value all the time. He led me to the car in Bundaberg – he said there was a steel grey one in Bundaberg, and to get on the computer and have a look. It was a two-owner steel grey one in very, very good condition.

About a year after Eric passed, he told me to get online and to join a chat room. I joined and started talking to this lovely man called Gary. I had taken a job as a nanny by that stage, and I was still trying to learn, with my spirituality really starting to take off. I was learning very quickly how to channel and how to become a medium and I had to decide at that stage whether I was going to become a professional medium, or whether to stay being a nanny or what I was going to do in life. I started getting many phone calls from people wanting me to do mediumship for them as they'd heard through friends and by word of mouth about what I could do.

Eric said to go and get another phone – a business mobile phone – so that I wasn't using my home phone. After I got the new mobile, I asked for another sign. I'd had another dream the night before that I was standing on a platform in space looking out and I saw the earth spinning. When I got this new mobile, I was messing around with it and somehow in the right hand corner a picture of the earth came up – there was this globe exactly how I'd seen it the night before in my dream. My fingers were just clicking away and somehow in the corner I got the earth. I thought, okay! This was still in 2001 and I knew there and then that I had to take on the spiritual journey because I was really able to understand what the spirits were trying to say to me and the information they were trying to relay to their loved ones. It was becoming very in-depth and very profound through telepathic pictures, images, senses, names, places, tastes... all kinds of things.

My personal life was moving forward too. Gary, the guy I'd started chatting online to, was a tradesman who lived on the north side of Brisbane. He had a daughter the same age as my son and we decided to meet. We had our first date at Redland Bay and we enjoyed each other's company – we spent the whole afternoon together and then had dinner. We would pick Luke up, take him to football and then spend the weekend at Gary's place. This continued for about six months, and during that time the Brisbane Sunday newspaper, *The Sunday Mail*, had got hold of me and wanted to do a big story on me, so I started to take off with the media side of things.

Gary is a huge AFL Brisbane Lions fan and we went to a dinner on the Sunshine Coast where the Brisbane Lions were having a charity event. I just knew that the famous AFL player, Jason Akermanis, was going to end up sitting at our table and I told Gary this. I was right. As Jason stepped forward, our table number was called. Jason was fascinated by what I was doing and had read the big article in the paper. I got to spend quite a lot of time getting to know him and his lovely wife and a friendship was formed.

Losing Mum

I had yet another huge loss coming up in my life. About a year after Eric had passed, I looked at my mother and had this gut-wrenching feeling of dread – the same gut-wrenching feeling I'd had with Eric. I knew something wasn't right. Not long after this feeling, my mum wasn't eating and had started to lose weight, and the doctors first diagnosed her as having some kind of a gut problem. They didn't diagnose it as cancer at first but my sister, brother and I knew that there was something more going on. Mum then went to another specialist who diagnosed her with stomach cancer. I just knew I was going to lose my mother. I felt my grandfather around and I felt Eric around, and it was like they were comforting me.

We continued to go up to the hospital and see Mum – my daughter and son had a very close bond with her and we would get up there as often as we could. The doctors decided to cut her whole stomach out and she had that major surgery, but by that time the cancer had spread through her body.

It was the same hospital and the same ward that Eric had been in just a year before – the Oncology Ward at the Princess Alexandra Hospital. Because I'd spent so much time up there with Eric, when I walked in there again the same doctors and nurses said, 'What are you doing up here again?' I pointed into the room and said that it was my mother, and they were just like, 'Oh, my gosh!'

Amanda's mother, Jackie

My mother continued to deteriorate to the point where she was not really with us – almost like a coma – and I knew she was connecting to me from the afterlife already. My brother, my sister, my dad and I organised to do eight-hour shifts so that someone was always with her. My father had been there and it was now my stint with Mum, with my brother coming in after me at midnight. Gary drove my father home, then came back to pick me up later when my brother turned up to take over from me. I kissed my mother good-bye and I just had this feeling that this was going to be the last time. I felt her say to me, 'I'm already gone. I'm not here anymore. I'm gone.'

Amanda's mother and father

I went back with Gary to his house. At 1am, we were both still awake and Gary's phone rang. It was my brother to say that my mother had just passed. We got up very early the next morning and decided that I would go and tell Dad as he didn't know at this stage, but I couldn't bring myself to tell my father that my mother had passed. Gary, being the strong one, held my father's hands and said, 'I'm sorry, mate, she's gone.'

The next week or two was a big blur but in a way there was a sense of peace around Mum. One thing I do remember about Mum's funeral was that it had been raining and Layla, Luke and I were sitting in the front row when all of a sudden this ray of sunlight came through the skylight and beamed down on us. Others saw this and commented on it.

My mother was very close to her five grandchildren and loved them all very much. My two children loved her dearly and spent a lot of time with her. She was a wonderful mother and grandmother and loved by so many.

ON THE MOVE

Gary and his daughter had wanted to move to the Sunshine Coast and we found a blue house in Eumundi with three acres of rainforest. It was perfect. Peter and I had parted ways formally by divorcing by that stage and he'd paid me out for my part of the house, so Gary, his daughter and I packed up and moved up to the coast.

We'd been living up there for about six months and I was extremely busy all the time. I had an office in Eumundi as *The*

Sunday Mail had done a two-page story about me with the journalist, Frances Whiting, and there was a second one that came out about a month after that which Jason Akermanis had written relaying the connection I'd made with him. My career was taking off, I had a lot of clients, and I was busy travelling. Sadly, Gary and I drifted apart because I was so busy and so engrossed in what I was doing and he was having his own dilemmas at that point. We went our separate ways and I bought the house off him.

A lovely man called Roger started to help me with my work around then. He was one of my first clients and he travelled with me for awhile as my first manager, but he had a lot of health problems and had things he wanted to do as well. We parted ways but I still stay in contact with him and will always be very grateful for all he did for me.

MY STUNNING TV DEBUT

I mentioned before about the universe starting to open many doors for me and my career taking off and starting to get a lot of media exposure. A big part of that was my appearance on the TV show, *A Current Affair*. It was amazing – both for me and for the people from the show! I think you'll agree after reading this.

A Current Affair had contacted me and made the appointment to come to my house. The crew turned up in the morning – a boom operator, a cameraman and the female interviewer who was quite sceptical. They had only been allocated two hours but ended up staying there all day! They skipped the other two appointments they were meant to have because they were so engrossed with what was happening with me.

First, the interviewer asked why I thought I was able to communicate. We'd only just sat down and I looked at the boom operator and said, 'Your grandfather – you have his middle name – is coming through. He's on your father's side and he died in a gun turret underneath a bomber when it hit a mountainside. His name was Wallace.' Well, the boom operator burst into tears. And even more amazingly, he was only allocated to be the boom operator that morning. He'd been called in at the last minute to do the story so there was no way I could've known anything about who he was. I went on to talk about his grandfather and the medal that they have at his house in the safe at the back where his wife is still living. They were recording all of this and the young lady interviewing me was quite stunned. She said to him, 'Is this true?' and he was crying and said, 'Yes, it's all true. He was killed in a gun turret when a plane hit the mountain. It was 50 years ago.'

We then tried to start the interview again and I turned around to the camera operator and said, 'Your grandmother has just recently passed. You were very close to her. And she wants you to know that your dream of owning a property and growing organic macadamias and avocados will come true.' Pretty specific information! And he just about dropped the camera. He said, 'Nobody knows that except my wife and myself and we've been talking about it for quite some time.' I said that this was around the Glasshouse Mountains and they were going to plant trees and have a farm. He broke down in tears because he knew it was his grandmother coming through and encouraging him to go for his dream.

We then tried for a third time to do the interview for the show. Lo and behold, I said, 'Hang on a second,' and by now the lady who was interviewing me was saying, 'Okay, what is going to happen now?' I said, 'Your grandfather tells me he used to live on a farm. You were in his farm truck when you were about three or four and you were mucking about when you accidently kicked the handbrake off. The truck started to roll down the hill and your grandfather leapt into it and pulled the brake on just before you were about to go into the dam.' Her reaction was utter shock. She said, 'My mother only just told me that story a month ago.' So the lady's grandfather came through and validated what I was doing by telling her something that I couldn't possibly have known. She'd been very sceptical when she walked in – they all were – but at the end of the day they weren't sceptical anymore!

The interviewer then decided that she was really going to put me to the test – they chose someone in the Sydney office for me to do a phone channelling with. I didn't even know this woman's name. I got onto the phone with her and all of a sudden I brought through someone. He told me his name, and he told me that he'd committed suicide and how he'd done it. I had learnt how to distinguish all of these details during my learnings which I'll speak more about later… but what a way to start a career! I said to her, 'Your husband is standing here, he committed suicide. You have two glasses of wine on the table at night. You still have a glass for him and a glass for yourself.' He told me how he passed, what he did around the passing, and he gave her so much validation. She was so shocked she went home from the office after that because I was so specific and spot-on.

A Current Affair then organised for me to go to the studio to test me out. They had a studio audience of about 20 people who'd been personally chosen by the staff, so it was some of the staff and their relatives and friends. I didn't have any prior knowledge of any of them. With the first young man I came to, it felt like a best friend was coming through and I said, 'You took a surfboard out after he passed.' This young man didn't look like a surfie guy at all and I said, 'He's laughing at you because you don't normally surf. You went to the beach and you paddled out on the surfboard and you took a wreath out and threw it in the ocean.' I saw that the guy who had passed over had a cancer in the leg and he had passed six months after it was detected. Another young lady had a pendant described to her by her father who'd given her this pendant which was a family heirloom. Then I communicated with the cameraman and his family and his dog came through too.

One lady had just walked into the studio at the back and I looked at her and said, 'Your close friend's son is coming through. He tells me his name is Matt and he was murdered.' And she was just shocked – she went white and I think she was about to pass out. She said, 'I was hoping. I heard about you through the corridors, everyone was buzzing, and I had to come and see for myself.' She had come through a back entrance and I went straight to her. Matt came through to connect to his mother and told her what had happened, about how he was beaten up in town on a night out with his friends. He told me it was in Cairns and that he had been in a coma for three or four days. I had most of the audience crying.

Then this same lady's father came through and told her that he had died three times and had had two near-death experiences. She validated this and said that he had died three times over two days from a heart attack. The third time he passed away. He talked about the near-death experiences of what he saw and she said, 'Yes, he told me what he had seen, and when he passed the third time I knew he wasn't coming back but I knew he was at peace because the two times he had the near-death experience, he told me he felt nothing but peace and he wasn't afraid.'

I was in there for nearly two hours, nobody wanted me to go, and even though it started off with 20 in the audience, large gatherings of people kept coming in. It was standing room only at the end.

So that appearance on *A Current Affair* (on Australia's Channel 9 Network) was my first real connection with a large media outlet and the first real respect I got from the media. Then came all the other media, so it went like a rollercoaster from there, for instance *Today Tonight* (Channel 7 Network) got involved and wanted to talk to me and ended up doing a story specifically about my animal communications. Nobody seemed to be able to fault me, as hard as they tried to test me.

I knew my life was never going to be the same and I embraced being catapulted into the public eye all of a sudden. I always remember and remind myself that this is not about me, this is not about celebrity or being famous or anything like that. I just love to do what I do because it brings such peace to people. I always remind myself that I need to stay grounded and humble – not that I need to do that often as

I'm generally grounded and down to earth anyway. People who know me know that I don't carry on like a public figure, expecting my own star trailer!

Another big step in my career, as well as a complete change of scenery, was about to take place. I got an opportunity to move down to Sydney where I had an enormous following. A national magazine had decided that my animal communications – which had started to take off by then – would be good for them as a regular feature. My first grandchild, Jacob, had been born to Layla by then and I decided that I would go to Sydney but would commute regularly, so I rented out my Eumundi house and rented a house in Sydney's North Rocks.

While in Sydney, I was invited onto the popular radio program, the Kyle and Jackie O Show. One day I was in the studio with them and all of a sudden I felt Kyle Sandilands' dog wanting to have a chat. Talk about spilling the beans on Kyle! As he put it – 'ratted out by my own dog'! The dog mentioned to me on national radio for all to hear that he wanted to thank his dad for popping into the Macca's drive-through and giving him the chicken nuggets while Kyle secretly chowed down on a burger and fries. It was so funny because Kyle was supposed to be on a diet at this time and he just could not get out of this one! Jackie O thought this was hilarious and Kyle had to own up to going to McDonald's for that burger almost every day and giving his dog the nuggets as a way of pay-off. But the dog didn't keep his mouth shut!

Even though Kyle is quite infamous for some of the things he has said over the years, I always found both him and Jackie O to be a lot of fun to be with and Kyle took the whole thing with his usual sense of humour. He treated me very well and with a lot of respect, as we had many callers wanting to connect to their pets and I was correct with all of my readings with the callers. One caller had lost his beautiful bird so I had a chat to him and told him where I felt it was and who had taken it. Kyle's staff rang me the next day to tell me they'd found the bird right where I said it would be, so my information was crucial to finding this beloved pet. This was just one of many such connections I've made while doing radio station interviews. I've always enjoyed them – making connections to the listeners and bringing through their pets and loved ones even though I have no idea who they are.

My beloved dog, Kelli, came into my life while I was in Sydney. I was home alone at night and decided I'd like a dog for the company and security. Kelli was bought from the RSPCA. When I first saw her, she told me her name was Kelli (they had actually called her Kelsey) and that she had a cold, which indeed she did. She was this cute little brown puppy and we connected immediately. I couldn't take her home at first because she had the cold and the RSPCA needed to make sure I had the right fencing as she was going to be a big dog. All went well and I got Kelli a few days later, and that was the start of our amazing journey together.

Kelli passed peacefully in my arms on the 14th of November, 2014. She was much more than a dog to me, with unconditional love from me to her and from her to me. The following day I took my other dog, Rommy, for a walk and out the corner of my eye I saw Kelli walking beside me as she always did. She was and still is an amazing, unique, gentle soul who was my rock for ten years.

Amanda's dog, Kelli

MICK

Unfortunately, life in Sydney became hard. I missed my children and was so homesick that I decided I was coming home. I only lived down there for four months and broke the lease on where I was renting. Luckily, the tenants renting my Eumundi house had bought their own home so I was able to move back in, much to the happiness of my children and Daggies. I was becoming very well known by that stage so I didn't feel that moving back to Queensland was going to badly affect my career in any way.

Amanda and Mick, 2005

Thank goodness I did move back because I was soon going to meet a man who would become a big part of my life for many years. My dear friend, Vicki, was having her birthday party in the Lockyer Valley, and for some reason I wasn't going to go, but ended up going and taking Daggies with me. There was this very tall, huge man standing on the other side of the table and I connected to him immediately. His name was Mick. We spent the evening chatting and had the most wonderful connection. He was from Adelaide and had his own truck so had to go away for work, but came back to Brisbane a week later. We spent five days together, then he had to go back again. He had a wicked, funny sense of humour and we connected on so many levels. We decided before he left to go away for two weeks that we wanted to be together. He got down on one knee after that third week and asked me to marry him! He had a ring in his hand –

it was a 17-diamond, blue sapphire ring that he had chosen. I said yes. I just knew.

In September, 2006, I had to fly to Canberra to work and then I flew to Adelaide to meet Mick. He sold his house and land and we drove back up to Brisbane. On the back of the road train (the prime mover and two trailers) was a Hilux utility, a caravan with all of Mick's bits and pieces in it, two carpenter trailers (he'd been a carpenter before a truck driver) and a container with personal items of his. Mick and I started our journey along with his 13 and 14 year-old children and a friend of theirs. There were two in the front and three in the bunk in the back and you'd have to lie down looking out if you were in the back. That was my first ever trip in a prime mover and it was certainly different! We did the two-day trek from Adelaide to Brisbane through Broken Hill, Wilcannia, Toowoomba and finally to Brisbane.

Mick's road train – one of many journeys together with Amanda

We stopped overnight and left the prime mover and two trailers at a friend's place in the Lockyer Valley. The kids, Mick, Kelli (who we'd picked up by this stage) and I piled into the Hilux ute and travelled up to Eumundi to my house to start our new life. The two kids hadn't originally intended to move but had come along for the trek and ended up deciding to stay. We went down and picked up the truck a week later and brought it up to Eumundi.

We found it very hard with Mick trying to work out of Brisbane so we moved out of the Eumundi house and rented a property in Greenbank near my father and my children. I sold the Eumundi house.

The Greenbank house we were renting eventually got sold so we had to move out of there next, and ended up going to Camira near Ipswich. In 2009 I decided to move out to be near my daughter and grandchildren at Minden in the Lockyer Valley. Mick stayed on in the Camira house with his children because it was convenient for him, but he was away a lot. I spent several trips with him in the road train from Brisbane to Adelaide and back, and loved being in the truck with him. We'd sleep in the truck and live in the truck – rain, hail or shine. I did about six or seven trips with him.

Mick's nickname for me was Chubb because I was a bit chubby! He always stayed in contact with the children and me, to let us know where he was and that he was okay on the road. I always helped him with the truck – with maintenance, changing tyres etc. I quickly learnt how to tarp and untarp, and I would get under the truck and grease it because I was much smaller than he was (he was six foot six and 137 kilos). It made his buddies laugh when I'd wheel out from under the truck on a trolley, this little blonde thing! I would help him a lot, getting parts for things, washing his clothes for him and sending him on his way again the next day with an esky of food.

I can tell you, there were some hilarious moments in that truck. I remember just outside of Cobar on the way to Adelaide, we had a road train of 70 tonnes and nearly 50 metres of truck and trailer – carrying steel and boats. It was coming onto dark and pouring with rain, and we had a blowout in one of the trailers so we pulled over. It was wet and muddy and we changed the wheel – we were both soaked, covered from head to toe in mud, and when we jumped back into the cab and looked at each other, we burst out laughing at the sight of each other! We were drowned rats and filthy dirty! But I loved it, and I loved having that time with Mick. He was an extraordinary and intelligent man and always a lot of fun to be around.

After I moved to be near my daughter who was having her third child, Mick and I lived separate lives but he would still come and see me and we still spent quite a lot of very precious time together. By this time, my career had really taken off and so much was happening, but Mick and I were still very close and had a very special bond. However, because I was away and he was away, sometimes we wouldn't see each other for weeks.

By now, Louise Corran had become my manager, taking over the running of my business, doing a new website for me, and organising events. We met at the Greek Club in Brisbane when I enquired about hiring a room to do a show. She worked there and we got talking and stayed in contact. Then Louise formed her own business, Packaged Events, and said that if I wanted her to organise events for me that she'd help me.

We had a discussion and it just went from there. We're really busy and she's just amazing. I could not have done all of this without her.

LOSING DAGGIES AND MICK

In the meantime, I had to deal with losing someone very dear to me. In early 2012, Daggies had to quit his job of over 25 years in the steel mill due to ill health. I watched his health deteriorate over the coming months as he had more time to spend at my place. He suffered a mild heart attack and was then not able to drive, so I would go and pick him up from his Brisbane home and bring him back to my place to stay with me for a few days. He was diagnosed with a severe heart problem and once again the feeling of dread was surfacing, but with Daggies I'd had a feeling and a knowing for quite some time.

In August 2012, Daggies spent a few days with me at my place and then I took him home. We had lunch at our favourite café and I kissed him goodbye, knowing this was going to be the last time I saw him. The next day he entered a private hospital for his major heart surgery. He only survived a few days and on 21 August, 2012, he passed away. He had suffered a lot of health issues for many years and I knew he was out of pain now. I miss my best friend of 23 years every day but I know he is still with me.

Just a year later in August 2013, it was to be Mick that I lost. I always had this feeling that he wasn't going to be around forever – that he would die young. He and I often discussed that I knew and he knew that he was not going to grow old. As a child he had been very sick, in and out of hospital for the first six years of his life with various illnesses, and when we were living in Greenbank he had survived cancer in the eye, which I'd nursed him through. Again, I had this horrible feeling of dread in August. I thought, *No please, not Mick, not Mick*. And I was overwhelmed with grief.

I saw him the week before he passed and his words were, 'Chubb, I've got a bad feeling about something.' And I hugged him and said, 'Please, please be careful because I know how tired you get in that truck and I know that you've been so busy.' I kissed and hugged him and told him I loved him. I then watched him drive off.

I constantly told him that week by text and phone, 'Please be careful', then this day I got a text from him at 4pm. It said, 'I'm that busy, Chubb, I can't scratch.' We had a lot of funny little sayings that we shared like that, a funny special language. One hour later at 5pm, Mick fell asleep at the wheel and was killed near Roma in Queensland. His truck rolled down 20 metres as he was driving on a range. He was 50 years old. That hour after he passed I just knew, and I was reliving those last eight years that we'd been together – our ups and downs, our very funny moments, our funny little ways with each other. I didn't formally know yet because I hadn't been notified, but I just knew inside. The next morning I got a phone call from Mick's son to tell me that his father had passed and how it had happened.

Three days before Mick passed, I'd had another profound dream. I saw myself standing over his body at a funeral chapel, and then when his funeral did happen and I went in to say good-bye to him, it was exactly like the dream. The whole surroundings of the chapel were exactly how I'd seen it all three days before he passed.

From the moment he passed, I knew Mick was still with me. I would laugh and cry because I would hear him and understand him. I remember things we used to do together, like getting my 2am 'raisin toast call'. He would text me at around midnight when he was near Toowoomba, saying, '2 am raisin toast, Chubb' which meant he wasn't far away and to defrost the raisin bread. I'd go and pick him up from the truck which he'd leave at a petrol station on the Warrego Highway, then bring him home in the car to have a long hot shower and raisin toast. He was usually so exhausted that he just wanted to sleep after that, then he'd have a big breakfast the next morning and I'd take him back to the truck so he could go to Brisbane to unload. Then I'd be given a huge bag of filthy dirty truck driver clothes to be washed! He always laughed when he gave them to me and would say, 'A present for ya, Chubb.' He was a Christian man, he loved God, and he was a very honest, deep person. I knew this man inside and out. He was huge and came across as pretty rough but I saw a side of him that very few other people saw.

Mick often brings music through to me – songs we used to listen to. At his funeral I stood up and did his eulogy, and ever since then I've just known he was around with music and songs and signs. In the truck, he often played and sang *Songbird* by Eva Cassidy to me and he makes sure I hear it a lot. Once was at breakfast with others at my Soul Rejuvenation Retreat at Maleny. Another time was at an event in Brisbane just after I came off stage and then another time it happened when I was driving home with my daughter. Layla thought it was strange as she hadn't remembered putting the song on her iPod. I know it's Mick as I feel him around when it's being played. I went to visit my best friend, Rebecca, on the Sunshine Coast for a bit of R and R, and when I walked into her house, Barry Manilow was singing *Mandy*. I knew that was from Mick too.

One time I brought Mick through to his son, and his son thought it was fantastic because I mentioned all the events that had happened in his life, even though I didn't know them myself. He knew it was his dad.

Just two weeks after Mick had passed, I had to go through another very sad experience concerning my dad. He'd been friends with a man named Frank for over 30 years. Mum and Dad played bowls with Frank and his wife and they were all good friends, but Frank's wife passed away about 15 years ago. When Dad was diagnosed with Parkinson's Disease and couldn't drive anymore, at least once a fortnight I would go and pick him and Frank up and take them both out for the day. I called them 'my two dads' and we'd go all over the place – from Mount Tamborine to the Gold Coast for a day out. Sadly, Frank passed over the same week that Mick did and his funeral was the day before Mick's. I had Frank's funeral at 2.30pm on the Tuesday and Mick's at 10am on the Wednesday.

During this time, I was also trying to deal with Dad and his constant falling over in his efforts to look after himself. We made a family decision to move him into respite care and get him into a nursing home permanently, which was a very hard decision for all the family. After 25 years of Dad being in the same house, my sister and I moved him out and cleared out the house. (This was happening only two weeks after Mick had passed.) It was hard to leave that family home after all that time and all of those memories. That was a very sad chapter in my life but I'm grateful I ended up having Dad in my life until very recently.

Despite those huge losses and challenges, life went on and mine continued to gain momentum. My daughter had three children – Jacob, Cooper and Lily – and my son had his first child, Hailee, with his long term partner Danni. My life was very busy with my children, my four grandchildren, my career and my father's ailing health.

Mick continues to this day to still be a part of my life and he still makes me laugh and brings through the funniest things, which is very typical of him. It always puts a smile on my face and cheers me up. He was a very peaceful and endearing man who will always have a place in my heart and there are so many funny, wonderful, outrageous memories of a truly amazing man. At the time of writing this I'm still living at Minden but Mick wants me to move up to the Sunshine Coast for the next part of my life.

Ten Interesting Things

As you've no doubt guessed by now, a lot of interesting things have happened to me! I've called this section TEN INTERESTING THINGS but a lot of the events are more than just interesting – they're very strange and powerful learning experiences that the universe has given me through events, dreams, my spiritual journey, and crossing paths with certain people. This includes my Ascended Master, Ashkiya. These events have all contributed to taking me to where I am today and they have helped make me the psychic medium and animal communicator that I am. It's all been a sequence of what I believe is not so much coincidences but more of a plan. As time goes on and more of these events and sequences and crossing of paths happen, I feel that none of them were accidental. Here we go!

One

When Eric passed, the doors really began to open up on my spiritual journey. The first day that he passed away,

I went back to my home and of course I was a complete and utter sobbing mess wondering how I was going to live without this special friend in my life. But then something wonderful happened. The first experience that I had was a feeling of knowing when Eric told me about some future experiences I was going to have. He showed me that he was in a place of peace – it was an overwhelming feeling of peace and something that I had never experienced before. I was awake and I could just feel my body feeling light and also a very strong, powerful feeling of tranquillity. It was almost like an out-of-body experience because what I was feeling was not me but him, Eric, trying to show me how peaceful it is 'over there'. I began to wonder where exactly he was (although I already knew at some level) and how I could connect to him on a more spiritual level, but I knew I was consciously connecting to him on a specific level. I didn't know how exactly, but as I've already told you I've known since I was a young child that there was something different about me and that I was going to be famous. I didn't really know what for, but I knew that as soon as Eric passed this new phase of my life was going to be opened – this new door and new chapter. This was the first day of that new beginning of my life. It was an overwhelming peaceful knowing and understanding. I thought, *I am now about to step into what I'm really meant to be doing.*

TWO

About two to three months after Eric passed, I had this feeling to go to a flea market and while there I picked up a brochure. It was for a workshop to bring out your spiritual abilities given by a man called Richard. I knew I had to go so I rang Richard and booked myself in. Richard said that the moment I walked in the door, he saw this magnificent golden light around me. Others saw it too. Richard had been in the industry for 45 years and he'd only ever seen it on three other people. He said, 'You have an incredible gift.' He knew it, and two other ladies – one was his partner – said exactly the same thing. I just knew this was where I was meant to be, even though I didn't have a clue what I was doing.

Meanwhile Richard was saying to me, 'You are a medium.' And I'm saying, 'I'm a what?' But I suddenly started to connect to this lady sitting beside me. I looked at her and I said, 'Your mother's passed over. You are waiting for a letter in a yellow envelope that is from OHMS like it's a government letter.' She nearly fell off her chair and choked on her Monte Carlo! And she said, 'Oh my gosh, yes, my mother has passed over.' I said, 'The letter is on its way and it's very good news and it's about a legal matter.' I didn't have a clue what I was doing – this was all new to me. She contacted me a few months later and said that the letter was exactly what I said it was. She knew after I'd told her that it would be alright because I'd said the letter would be in her favour.

THREE

I started to do some readings for people who would come to my home, and one lady asked me to come to her spiritual church to tell people my story. By this time I was being fed information and was starting to meet Ashkiya and Eric and my grandfather, and they were starting to help me open up my spirituality and abilities which I knew were there by that stage.

Richard had told everyone about me and my gift and I was getting offers from all over the place – Toowoomba, Gympie and other places – with all these spiritual churches wanting me to go there. But it was early days and I was working as a nanny, not sure about where I was heading.

At this spiritual church, I sat in the front row and they called me up and again I still didn't know what I was doing. Up at the front I said, 'Hello, my name's Mandy and I've just started this journey of spiritualism and mediumship.' All of a sudden I went, 'Who owns Ella? Ella was killed in a car accident.' I could feel like my body was lifting and I could see in my mind what she was saying to me. She was killed in a car accident, there were four cars involved, it was at Christmas time, she was in a small white car, it was on a freeway, it was in another city, there was a truck involved, she was someone's sister and she bought her a clock, it was circular and it pointed outwards like a moustache, and it was in the back seat of the car and she had a necklace on, and she and her sister had exchanged necklaces the Christmas before. This lady in the back row, Catherine, started to cry and said, 'My sister was Ella and she was killed in a car accident.' And everybody was gobsmacked with my precise information.

I did a couple of other readings that night that were also quite profound. Another lady's husband had come through and was laughing that the fence was falling down and had rather a large bow shape. He told her to fix the fence and gutters if she was going to sell the house. She was also quite shocked to hear this as she was thinking of selling the house and had told no-one.

I got Catherine's number and several people came up to me and said, 'How much do you charge to do a reading?' and my dumbfounded answer was, 'What? What do you mean charge?' I had no idea. I went to work as a nanny the next week.

On the Friday night, I was woken up by Ella at 11pm. I woke up to see Ella's face in my face and she was saying urgently, 'Ring her, tell her to stop it! Ring Catherine, dangerous, dangerous! She's got a tomato shaped sauce bottle and she's got the Ouija board, she's trying to contact me.' I had Catherine's number so I got up and rang her. I said, 'Catherine, I'm so sorry, it's Amanda here and Ella is here with me and she is jumping up and down terrified. I woke up and her face was in my face and she was literally screaming at me. Are you putting sauce into a sauce bottle shaped like a tomato?' She said, 'Oh my gosh, yes!' And I asked if she'd been trying to contact Ella through a Ouija board since my connection with her and she said yes, she was contemplating it. She had got the board out but had not used it yet. I told her that Ella was screaming at her, 'Do not use the Ouija board!' I was still half asleep at this stage after being woken up out of a sound slumber with a dead person screaming in my face and in my ear. So I warned her, 'Do not do it, Ella is frightened, you will bring in a spirit, you do not know what you are doing. Please throw away the Ouija board.'

Again I made Catherine cry but good tears, and I felt a sense of authority around me, like a respect from the afterlife, a respect from my Guides and a respect from people who were beginning to know who I am. Very quickly I was learning how to channel and to understand the concept and the language of my beautiful Guides, including my grandfather, Ashkiya and Eric.

FOUR

I have received some amazing lessons from my Guides. Eric is one of my Guides whereas Mick is more a supporter than a Guide. These days I have 11 very, very powerful Ascended Masters including Ashkiya and over 170 Spirit Guides for the many different gifts that I have, including healing, mediumship, body talk, animal communications and so on. I started off with my main Ascended Master, Ashkiya, and gradually one by one they have all joined me. Ascended Masters are different from Spirit Guides and teachers; they are supreme beings of pure love and intelligence and are generally given to people in this line of special work. They are on a different, much higher level and oversee the Guides and the teachers. None of my 11 Ascended Masters have ever been human whereas Spirit Guides have often lived a human life.

In that time after Eric passed and the spiritual doors opened to me, Ashkiya started to show me lives I've had in the past – with many lives of spirituality as a healer, animal lover and also being burnt at the stake as a witch in England. I began to find out my soul history, which was very interesting to say the least, but I already knew about many of these past journeys. I associated, understood and really connected with each and every one of my previous lives – from a German soldier to a Tibetan monk to an Hawaiian healer to an English doctor, and of course the witch. Some were simple lives but some were of notoriety, so my soul history was a diversity of different characters and lifestyles, from a poor person living in India to a privileged person in Egypt.

One life in particular was in America with the Indian Appaloosa horses. I connected to these war horses and

I was the main keeper of these amazing creatures. I also remember two Aboriginal lives that I had in the Dreamtime – anyone who knows me knows that I love the Aboriginal people and their Dreamtime and have a great respect for their culture. I also had three Egyptian past lives – twice as a healer (the king's and a family's) and once as a cat lover in the palace. In this current life when I went to Egypt with my mother on our way to England, I entered one of the pyramids and had this very comfortable feeling of being at home.

FIVE

As I began to connect with Ashkiya, she began to teach me how to telepathically communicate with her. My body would sleep but my soul would be taken to where I needed to learn – I guess you'd call it astral travelling. During these journeys, I was taken to a place called the Universal University, which has massive, creamy stone-like buildings – like any older university but on a much larger scale. The size of the university probably would've taken up the whole city of New York. I remember sitting near the lake – Ashkiya would sit me on a park bench and I would see the university, the people, the sheer beauty and grandeur of this amazing place. Ashkiya would be at one end of the bench which was about two metres away from me, and I was up the other end overlooking the park and the lake. It was just beautiful.

The lake area had all kinds of animals in it roaming free – monkeys, bears, horses and an array of other beautiful animals. I felt them all near me and around me and they weren't afraid. They were the souls of animals, some of them extinct, and I could see them. I remember there was this Chinese warrior and he came up to me while I was sitting on this bench.

I was looking at him and he sat in front of me, bowed his head and looked at me. He had a ponytail and was in full war regalia, and he said to me, 'I am your second Ascended Master.' He looked like one of those entombed warrior statues and his name was Chi Lang. He showed me a life that I had had with him where I had been an empowered (male) emperor. Somehow I felt very peaceful around Chi Lang and I felt protected from any dark or violent energy, a psychic attack, or any negative energies. He just sat there quietly and I know he's still with me to this day.

SIX

In another of my astral travelling learnings during my sleep, Ashkiya gave me a book about spiritual soul journeys and I read it in my mind and transferred what I was reading to her. She then said in a telepathic way back to me what I had just read to her. Ashkiya was validating to me what I was interpreting to her from this book, although she could not see the book, nor did she know the contents of the book. This was how I learnt to telepathically communicate. I was learning from the book what I was reading but I was also learning to interpret. I started to communicate with the animals in the same, interpreting way that I was connecting to Ashkiya through the book, but I knew it was a slightly different language for the animals so that they could understand everything I was saying – to the horses, the bears, the monkeys etc. Ashkiya and I then reversed – Ashkiya read something from the book in her mind, interpreting it to me in my mind, and I then telepathically said back to her what she had read in her mind to me. I got ten out of ten for that!

This went on for three nights, and one night I had just basically come back to my body and looked down and saw my body fast asleep in my bed. I was still in the Jimboomba house at this stage and Eric had not long passed. I remember floating back down into my body and getting some sleep to go to work the next day. The pattern would be that I would have three days of learning and then some time off to go through my mental notes. I would then be taken again for another three days of learning. This went on for several years and still goes on to this day if there is something that needs to be taught to me.

SEVEN

The next three-day learning was the Book of Akashik Records, which is a book of everybody who's ever lived on this planet and anybody who will ever live, so basically it's an endless book. Ashkiya took me to a very open place, almost like a stadium, and I was taken to this stage. I stood next to Ashkiya and I could see in the distance a very, very old man with a very long beard. He was crippled over and was standing in front of this huge, massive book which was thousands and thousands of years old. It was gold and faded, very thick, and it had a hard cover with *Akashik Records* written across it.

There was a line of tens of thousands of people and they all had a key and I also had a key. Every single one of those people put their keys in and nothing happened. Over the three days, anticipation built up and the line was getting shorter and shorter and I could see myself every night getting closer to this record book. I knew this book had something to do with me.

On the third night, it was my turn. I put the key in, I turned the lock, and the whole book flew open! I was the only one out of maybe 70,000-80,000 people who had been able to open the book. This golden light flew up out of the book and enveloped me, Ashkiya and the old man. The pages on the left hand side were the people who had passed over and the old man looked at me and pointed, saying, 'Many of those people you will connect to for their loved ones living.' He then pointed to the right side of the book and said, 'You will also connect to thousands and thousands of people who will pass over time and people still living and going to be living.' I felt a knowing that what he was saying was true and I just stood there with Ashkiya who was smiling. I knew that Chi Lang was still there keeping an eye on me too. I stood in awe of this book and I touched it and felt this enormous power going through me – not an egotistical power, it's never been egotistical; it's always been a knowing. I looked over and I saw Eric, my grandfather and my grandmother. I could smell my grandfather around – I could smell tomatoes (remember my grandfather was a gardener). I just knew that this was what I was meant to do.

Ashkiya continues to take me to the Universal University, that physically exists in the other realm which isn't the human realm. It is an actual group of large, old buildings. When I go there, she will telepathically tell me where to meet her and when I come to the university it's like my soul travels to it and I hover to it; my body sleeps but my consciousness and my soul travel through a portal – it only takes me a matter of half a second to get there. I look down on it and Ashkiya will say to me, 'I'm in the library' or 'I'm in the park at the front near the lake' or she might be right over the other side in the museum, and I will track and find her and sit with her, and she teaches me.

Eight

Ashkiya doesn't teach me everything – sometimes she will bring in Guides and teachers to teach me lessons about how to be a professional medium, for instance how to deal with raw human emotions of people who are just falling apart because you've just connected to their passed-over child or their mother or father. You have to learn every facet of dealing with human emotions, such as the grief and the anger. You have to learn how to bring it through in a warm, loving and sincere way. You're dealing with raw human emotions and you have to be taught etiquette and the right way to say things, how to deal with difficult people, angry people, media, clients and sceptics. You are taught everything in that university, but nothing prepares you for the real thing in real life.

Sometimes I would go to the medical section of the Universal University where Ashkiya would meet me. I would look at the human body and begin to learn body talk – the skeletal, the muscular, internal organs. They showed me every part of the human body. I would have to learn through body talk and then I started to learn to connect to people's bodies and how to heal. This is how I'm now able to determine through body talk what is wrong with a person – if they've had a health problem or if they might be unable to conceive etc.

In the university, there's also the Death Department – and I know it sounds morbid – but it was there that I was taught how to correctly diagnose a death… how someone has died, whether it be that you translate a picture of a car accident, or translate a picture of a heart attack or a suicide. I learnt to diagnose and decipher every possible way of passing.

For instance, I'd see a bowel and see black and I would see either a tumour or cancer, so I was then able to determine that they passed away from cancer in the bowel. For a stroke, I'd see blood from the left ear to the right chest. I would see black in breasts for breast cancer or I would see drowning. As well as deciphering, I feel what the passed-over people feel for a split second – but it does not impact me physically.

NINE

As part of these teachings, I then learnt about the family – how to decipher which family member is coming in. For example, directly above and to the right of a person having a reading I would sense a male figure – the father. Directly above to the left would be the mother. Halfway between the person and the mother I would see siblings. I always knew what family member was coming through, whether brother, sister, child or grandparent. Then I learnt to decipher how long they had passed, so I would get a gauge – every 5, 10, 15, 20 years. I would know that this person had been gone ten years on the gauge then I would get the Guides from the Death Department coming in. I would see the length of time and who it was who'd died and then the reason for passing. I would know all of this in a matter of a few seconds.

The next department was the Personality Department. I would say to the person, 'Your brother had a great sense of humour, he loved football, he was very cheeky, he used to pull your hair as a child.' So I learnt the personality of the passed-over person and to understand and interpret the messages that they wanted their loved one to know. And that wasn't just with humans but with animals as well.

I was shown that there are two different types of passing – 'prolonged passing' and 'trauma passing'. A prolonged passing is usually a person who's been sick for some time and is more than happy to make the journey home to the afterlife. This transition is usually very smooth as they are ready and prepared, and there are always loved ones waiting for them when they pass. A trauma passing is someone who's passed suddenly and unexpectedly, which could be from an accident or heart attack or anything else sudden. A trauma passing can obviously be a bit of a shock to the person as they were definitely not expecting it. There are always loved ones there waiting for them too as it can take a little while for the trauma passing to settle back in, especially if they were not expecting it, but they always do settle in and have lots of help to make this happen.

I was also taught how to understand grandparents on which side, great grandparents going back through many descendants, grandchildren, children, other relatives and friends. They all have a specific space on that relationship gauge. I can also interpret unborn babies – miscarriages and terminations – and stillborn babies. They can come through and they do. I can also interpret messages for loved ones from a spirit that is not directly connected to the person having the reading, but the person may know a family member to whom the message needs to be passed on. For instance, this could be your best friend's brother or your work colleague's wife coming through, because if they have a chance to get a message through they will just to let their loved ones know they are okay 'over there'.

I had to learn and study all these different departments, which probably took 18 months to two years with these three-night learnings once every two weeks or so in the beginning.

While it was happening, I knew I was being prepared for something big and I worked hard for it. This was about 2004 and over that time I had gained momentum and a whole lot of respect.

TEN

I was very overwhelmed by the responsibility that was now bestowed on me as I knew this was something not just national but international, and that I was being prepared to be thrust out into the public for scrutiny. But I knew I had to do this and was never afraid.

One night, Ashkiya took me to a platform above the earth and I looked through the portal and I could see the universe and the Universal University and I knew that that was the afterlife. Eric came to this glass-like portal about a metre in diameter with a platform just below it (but I was hovering in space) and he said to me telepathically, 'They need you and that planet needs you.' I said, 'I want to go home' and Eric said, 'You came back kicking and screaming this time but you know that you had to go back because you're so needed and it's your journey. You are the best and you know that.' Ashkiya turned me around, I looked at planet earth rotating and she pointed at it and said telepathically, 'They need you. You've been sent back there for a reason. You will become very well known and sought after, and that planet needs you to restore peace and to bring peace.'

Ashkiya then brought in several more Ascended Masters to the platform for me to meet and connect to. I still had Chi Lang and Ashkiya and my Spirit Guides, but suddenly I became aware of seven more Ascended Masters. I turned around on the platform and I said, 'I will do this, I will take this on.' And I knew I was sent back here to earth for a powerful reason.

After I had learnt everything from all the different departments of the Universal University, which probably took just over a year, I remember sitting on a seat waiting for Ashkiya and thinking, *What's next?* She handed me what seemed to be a scroll of paper and then I felt my Guides and Ascended Masters around me as she said, 'You've learnt all that you need to learn. You need to go out there and make a difference now.' It was like she handed me a certificate… like I'd graduated. There was no big fanfare but I heard cheering in the background – even though I couldn't see anyone. Then all of a sudden I saw all my Guides around me and I was a little nervous. I thought, *Now I've got to go out there and prove myself.* I just felt this gentle push from Ashkiya and it was like, 'It's okay, I'm here. I'm still here as your teacher, your professor, your mentor.' Ashkiya promised she would never leave me and she never has, and I am being told this is my last trip back here to earth.

My Ascended Masters now help me through every aspect that I need them for – some are for healing, some are to help me with certain readings and so on and some are to teach me composure and to keep my cool – they've all got their specific purpose. Two are for healing and body talk, another three are for animals, and another two are for my own personal use, so to speak, to keep me grounded and help me through with energy. One is to send me love, peace and energy to help me get through my readings, because it takes a lot of energy to do what I do at the pace I go.

CONNECTIONS

Interpreting what comes through

I've told you about how I learnt to interpret who is coming through with my connections to people and animals so now I'll give you some specific examples of how this has worked. I can receive messages any time and any place – I know they are messages for me and who they are from, and I may be driving in the car or even hanging out the washing. I know the difference between my grandfather, my mother, my Guides and my powerful Ascended Masters and the celebrity souls (more about them later). People are always fascinated about what I actually see, hear and feel and they always have a lot of questions for me so I'll explain it further.

When people come through, I ask them how they passed and I might get a vision, a physical feeling, a sense of something that's happened… or they will show me themselves how they passed. For instance, I saw a man who showed me that he was shot in the chest. I saw the shotgun, I saw where it happened, and I saw it was his brother who shot him. The person having the reading knew that the one brother who was mentally ill had come to the house and shot the other brother point blank at the door of their farm, so what I had seen was validated.

With vehicle accidents I feel the impact. I see the single car or the two cars collide. I see the circumstances around that passing – whether there was alcohol involved, whether there were several people in the car, and if there was speeding involved etc. One involved four young teenagers who were tragically killed in an accident and nobody knew why it happened. One of the teenagers, the driver, came through and showed me what happened and many questions were answered for the grieving parents of those children.

With a missing person, who could be dead or alive, I say to the person wanting the reading, 'Be prepared for whatever I bring through and if you aren't then I'm not going to go on with the reading.' No one has walked out yet and many mystery missing person cases have been solved.

Sometimes, if it's a missing person or people are unsure how their loved ones or pets passed over, their loved ones or pets will show me what happened. They will point to a specific part of their body – so with a heart attack I feel tightness in the chest and a sudden passing. They also show me where it happened, for instance they might've been lying in bed. One person showed me he had a heart attack at a set of lights in his car.

As I've said previously , if it's cancer they show me cancer in the body, which I see as black. So if it's in the lungs or the bowel, I see black or a tumor through that part of the body.

They also tell me the timespan of how long it took for them to pass and if there was a misdiagnosis or an undiagnosed illness, whether the reason for passing was unknown, sudden, unexpected or definitely expected. I feel not just the passing but all the circumstances surrounding that passing.

SOLVING MYSTERIES

I often help solve mystery passings. One man was on his boat and he showed that the boat had exploded. The family knew that but they didn't know how or why it did. He showed me a leak in a pipe which had made the boat explode. Another mystery was a helicopter accident. Nobody could figure out what had happened and the family hadn't been given an explanation. The man came through and told me what had happened from the moment he got out of bed that day to the afternoon when the accident occurred. The incident was under investigation at the time and the family were not really allowed to be told everything. I wasn't telling them anything that they weren't allowed to be told, but just what the passed-over man wanted them to know, which did give them plenty of closure.

Once with an American lady from Philadelphia who I'll call L, her mother and father came through but very separately. I saw her father shoot her mother in the head through the car window and then shoot himself in the head. L knew the basics – that her father had shot her mother and then himself – but she wanted to hear it from her father. There were a few questions that L needed to ask her mother, and thank goodness the woman hadn't seen it coming. She was in her car and by the time she'd lifted up the garage door and was attempting to flee, her husband had gone back into the house, loaded the gun, ran to her car, and shot her as she was backing out looking the other way. So she wasn't aware of what was about to happen.

L travelled from the other side of the world to visit me in Sydney for that reading because she needed to know the truth, which she got. She'd heard about me through another American lady in Philadelphia who had originally heard about me through a relative in Australia. She'd had a reading and was so impressed with it that she told L, who also heard a CD of the reading, some of which had information about her in it, so she knew that I was very accurate. L's sister found out I was going to Sydney and immediately booked a flight for her from the U.S. Let me tell you, there was a lot of closure for that lady and her family, both here and passed over.

SUICIDES AND MURDERS

Usually people who commit suicide come through and talk about the circumstances of what tipped them over the edge, and they also let me know if they left notes. Some are out of the blue and totally unexpected, as in one young man who missed his mum so much after she passed that he just didn't want to be here anymore although he didn't tell anyone at the time.

Nearly all of the suicides are met by loved ones passed over who are aware of what happened or is about to happen, and they group around that person to support him or her as obviously they've gone over because of an emotional trauma. Some have suffered depression for a long time or are bipolar, or something has happened in their past that they just can't deal with anymore because it's too hard and traumatic for them. When that happens, they always come through and talk it through with their family and say, 'This is how I was really feeling.' They never lay blame on anyone or want their loved ones to feel angry at themselves, because a lot of the time the family members feel they themselves are to blame.

Murders are of course very traumatic events for the loved ones of the victim. I've done a few readings of people who have been murdered – and I won't divulge their identities – in some cases helping the police investigation, starting with the case of a young man who was killed in Victoria in about 2004. His mother came to me and ended up taking the CD of the reading I did with her son to the police. The young man said where he had been found and described being thrown into the creek and his body being wedged under a railway bridge which looked like a miniature shape of the Sydney Harbour Bridge. He had a comb in his pocket (which was not generally known), he had an indentation of a ring in the top right side of his forehead from the hit, and he was weighed down by three different things – a besser block, a red brick and a rock – and I saw all of this in detail. It helped the police understand who'd committed this crime and why, as he also described the three men who murdered him and even the car that they drove. My information led to the conviction of one of the three men.

One lady, K, had a reading with her best friend who'd been murdered by her husband who had apparently gotten away with it.

The first thing the murdered woman said to her best friend was, 'Thank you for the beautiful red rose that you placed at my gate after I passed.' Nobody knew that except K – she did put a red rose at the gate of her friend's house after the murder. The next thing she said was, 'You're right, he had me murdered.' The passed-over woman then went through how her husband had done it. K knew instantly that this man had murdered her friend and she took the CD of my reading with her to the police. They gathered more evidence but they still couldn't prove that he did it. The policeman rang me afterwards and said, 'How did you know all that stuff? You could not possibly have known. I wish that a medium's information was submissible in courts.'

Because of my reputation of having helped with murder investigations, the police approached me about a triple murder case. The three murdered people came through and told me that whoever did this had been to a petrol station just before this had happened and that the person was in a white van around the corner from the house. Now I had no idea where this house was or anything else about the case, but the police found a receipt from the petrol station on the ground, and there had been a white van involved connected to the fuel receipt. I had told the police where to look for the receipt, which they found, and this helped with their investigations, with the suspected person eventually being arrested and convicted. The murder victims also showed me that their murderer had come in near a creek, then came into the house at the back, had gone up into the manhole and was watching through the roof. Sure enough, in the roof the police found some paper and evidence that someone had been up there recently.

So in general, the people show me how they pass and the circumstances surrounding how they pass. If it's suicide by hanging, I see the hanging or if for instance a man jumps off a building, I might feel that jumping and falling and then an impact. These types of details are what the universe taught me to understand in my lessons.

PHYSICAL AND MENTAL AILMENTS – DO THEY DISAPPEAR?

People who have passed over like to clear a lot of things up about their passing, like whether it's a trauma passing or a prolonged passing. As I explained earlier, prolonged passing is, say an elderly person or a person who's been sick a long time, who's just given up. They're ready to go, they've had enough, their body is in pain, and they are just happy to make the transition.

It might seem obvious but I want to stress that they do not take the physical problems over with them. The cancer or ailments stay with the physical body – that includes dementia, cancer, heart problems or any physical problems. It should give a lot of people comfort who've had the heartbreak of a loved one not knowing them because of dementia that patients come through as they were before the dementia. I find elderly people fascinating when they come through because they love to talk about their lives – who they were and what they loved.

When people who've had mental challenges come through, the intellectual disability is not there and they come through as a normal soul. With people who have multiple personalities, what I see are many different souls in the one body. So when that person has passed over, there is only one true soul left. They will come through and show me that they had multiple personalities, and I feel that this is also a physical thing as well, but I see the multiple souls. Once that body has ceased to exist, then the true original soul comes through without the other personalities. They attached themselves to the person but there is also a physical thing with the brain. It's almost like the brain has all these personalities in it and there are souls to match these personalities, and it can lay dormant for quite a long time.

One young man who'd passed over took his own life because of this. He said to his mum, 'They were there from the day I was born but every so often you would see them surface.' All of a sudden, they would just take over and he wouldn't be able to control them. When he passed and the physical body ceased to exist, those other souls left and what came through was just him and his true beauty which his mother immediately recognised. He was the original inhabitant of that body.

As you can see, there is no such thing as intellectual disability or physical challenges after death. Many times I've had people come through who had been challenged through disability but they always let go of that physical or mental disability and their true soul comes through. I've told you about my best friend, Peter – Daggies. He was only slightly Down Syndrome so he was still able to work and drive and lead a pretty normal life. Since he's passed over, when he's come through to me he's still himself and I know it's him but the Down Syndrome has left. He guides me and I get a slightly different feeling from him, but he's still got that great sense of humour and that fun-loving way about him. He used to call me 'Fat Bum' (which I never minded)! I'd get a message on my phone saying, 'Hello Fat bum, it's just me, call me back'. He still calls me that even though I've lost a lot of weight! He doesn't care about that. To him, I'll always be Fat bum!

COMMUNICATING WITH THE UNCOMMUNICATIVE

People often ask me about connecting with people who are alive but who are uncommunicative because of a physical disability – whether they have Cerebral Palsy, Alzheimer's Disease or are in a coma or whatever the circumstances are. In these cases, I can connect to the uncommunicative person's soul and bring through messages to loved ones. When they're in that state of what you could call 'suspended limbo', their soul tends to lift out of their body. This is why people know what is happening when they're having a near-death experience or an operation or if they've had an accident – their body shuts down but they're still able to be aware of what's going on as their soul sees it all. In a way their soul is floating above the body, and even though the body still exists it shuts down so there's no response from the body. That's when you get people being able to talk about what happened during an operation or a car accident etc., and having an out-of-body experience.

The same thing happens when I communicate with people who are non-communicative. Over the years of their lives, Alzheimer's sufferers, disabled people and so forth have been able to slip in and out of their body, so to speak, and communicate with me almost like a soul who has passed over. Although it's not a detached soul; it's an attached soul. They're able to bring through information to me that they want to pass onto their loved ones even though their body is still functioning.

For example, cancer patients who have gone into that comatose state in the final few days of life are no longer in that body – they're hovering above that body. Their soul flips out of their body and they're able to tell me all kinds of things that have happened when people have come to visit them to say good-bye or people who've combed their hair or read to them – they're able to give that loved one still living that validation to know that they were there, even though their physical body had shut down. Their spiritual self was well aware, alert and able to see what was going on. They will also tell their loved ones that other loved ones who have passed over are there to take them back home.

If you've got a dementia or Alzheimer's patient, they adapt themselves to flip in and out of their body any time they want to, so they know what's happening around their family. They're not allowed to go too far away from their body because it's still functioning and they still have to come in and out of their body and are very much aware of what's going on. If you've got an elderly lady with Alzheimer's whose husband has passed over, she'll be with her husband and she'll come through with him. But she's not allowed to go over to the afterlife until her body ceases to exist. When her body has taken her last breath, then that cord can be cut and she'll be free to go over to the afterlife.

An Alzheimer's patient will tell me what is going on with them physically and they'll be able to tell me what has been happening with the family. They themselves can't wander too far from the body but they're told by other passed-over loved ones what's going on with the family, because they (the ones who have passed over) visit the family and report on them to the one still connected to their body.

One lady who'd suffered from Alzheimer's for many years and had been in a nursing home in Sydney said to her daughter via my connection with her, 'I know you took my wedding rings off and I know that you put them in a small, round glass container. It was a cut glass container.' Nobody knew this but her daughter. The woman also said, 'I know that you took my wedding rings off because you were frightened of them falling off my hands.' Sure enough, the daughter had taken off the weddings rings, taken them home and put them in a small, round, cut glass container with a lid on it. Her passed-over father saw her do that and came back to the mother and told her, 'J has taken your rings.' Through this, the mother saw her take the rings and heard her say, 'I'm sorry Mum, I don't mean to take your rings but I'm taking them for safekeeping.' So this lady, J, had a communication with her Alzheimer's-suffering mother who specifically told her that she knew about the rings and that her father had said why and where she'd put them. Nobody else knew this so it was validation.

She also said to her daughter, 'Thank you for buying me the CD player and all those lovely CDs with the old English and Irish songs that you play to me. I love them and thank you very much for them.' So, this lady knew that her daughter had only recently bought her a CD player and CDs and that she'd asked the staff to play them for her mother, which they did. Even though she was basically not there most of the time because of the advanced Alzheimer's, she knew what was going on.

Another recently passed-over lady came through after she'd been in that three-day stage of hovering – her body had shut down and she was in the last phase of transition from life to death. When she came through, she said to her daughter, 'Thank you for reading the verses from the Bible on my last day.' And in fact her daughter had sat there for probably two or three hours and had read a small Bible to her mother, then had tucked the Bible underneath her mother's pillow and asked God, 'Please take my mother gently because we love her very, very much.' This woman was unconscious by that stage – she had been for three days – but she knew that her daughter had read her those verses and had put the Bible under the pillow.

ABORIGINAL CONNECTIONS

I have always had a huge respect, love and understanding of the Aboriginal ways. On many occasions my love of the Aboriginal people has seen me connect to passed-over elders and I have a respect and an understanding of their love of this land. I've always been drawn to the Aboriginal Dreamtime and mesmerised by their dancing and artwork, and I know I've had past lives as an Aboriginal and will always hold those past lives close to my heart. In actual fact, two of my main Guides are Aboriginal and I love them both dearly.

When I lived in Eumundi, my house was on three acres of rainforest. This area had apparently been a tea plantation at some stage. When I first moved in, I was aware of the female Aboriginal elder, Mary. Mary was often around my house keeping an eye on me and making sure I was safe, and I still feel her around to this day. She had lived and worked on the property many years ago when it was a tea plantation.

FAMILIAR CONNECTIONS

I have made some wonderful, enduring connections over the years – not just to some of my clients but also to their loved ones who have passed over. These beautiful souls are like family to me, as I've been connecting to some of them for many, many years and know them so well. They always have something different to say each time they connect, and I also enjoy communicating to them repeatedly as it's like talking to family and catching up. I feel a familiar soul coming through with some of them that have been a part of my journey from the beginning.

FAMOUS CONNECTIONS

People are often fascinated when they find out I've had several connections with passed-over people who were famous in their earthly lives, so I wanted to share with you some of those very special connections and why I feel these souls share their information with me. Some of them have come through because people who've known them have had a reading from me, and sometimes they just come through to teach and guide me. If this is the case it's because they are still here to help me. It is never about them anymore – the reason they are here is to help me on my journey. I never look at them as famous people as this is not the level of connection I have with them. I look at them as my mentors and Guides, and many of them are a continuing part of my life on so many levels.

Of course some sceptics like to mock people like me when we say that we've spoken to someone famous in the afterlife, but to the question of why someone famous would connect to me, I'd then ask the question, 'Why not someone famous?' Because they're not famous once they've passed over, and I feel that it's because of their fame and the pitfalls of having to deal with fame that they have some very valuable lessons to teach me about living in the public eye.

I'm not comparing myself to someone with the level of fame of Princess Diana or AC/DC lead singer, Bon Scott, but nevertheless I'm out there in the public and under scrutiny. So, here are some insights about some of the famous people I've had the pleasure of connecting with.

PRINCESS DIANA

The amazing, beloved Princess Diana – the people's princess. Who can ever forget her? My connection with her soul came when I was living at Eumundi. Out of the blue, for some reason I felt Princess Diana around – it was a very strong sensation. She did not come through as high or mighty; it was just a beautiful, gentle energy.

I didn't understand why she'd be coming through to me because there would be no way I could get a message through to her sons or family, but I knew it was her.

My partner at the time, Gary, and I were driving to Noosa and I said, 'Princess Diana's here', and he looked at me for a moment like I had three heads! But he also knew me so of course he didn't discount it. He said, 'Why is she here?' I said, 'I feel like there's something about one of her sons.' As we got closer and closer to Noosa, I just felt her get stronger and stronger. She wanted me to know that she was there. For some reason I felt we should turn on the radio, which we did and wouldn't you know it, we immediately heard that Prince Harry had just made a surprise visit to Noosa and was having a swim not five minutes from where we were!

I knew that Diana wasn't asking me to try and talk to Prince Harry but I also knew that she needed me to know she was there for… as she put it 'future reference' – which has now become clear because I can talk about it for this book! Obviously, we couldn't get anywhere near where Prince Harry was but I could sense Diana's love for her son, and she knew that I knew she was there. She's a beautiful, gentle, loving nurturing soul, still loving her sons from beyond the grave, and she needed me to know that she was still around her children and knew where they were.

Incidentally, I recently read an article about Prince William's and Kate's family dog since the new little Prince has been on the scene, and I can tell you that this regal dog was quite happy to share the information with me that it has seen a certain beautiful lady hovering around the palace.

Kerry Packer

I was working for one of media magnate Kerry Packer's many magazines doing an animal communications column. I was still up at Eumundi and it was probably a couple of weeks after Kerry Packer had passed over. I felt this very strong, no-nonsense presence around me – Kerry has got this 'Sit down and let's get this job done!' type of presence. (Even while I'm telling you about these people, I'm feeling them around.)

In my house my bedroom was upstairs, and this particular night my motion detector light kept flicking on and off. You'd hear the *click, click, click, click*. I knew that there was a presence around. At 2am, my smoke alarm went off and at first I thought it might've been Mary, the beautiful Aboriginal elder I've mentioned who was like a guardian around my house, but it just didn't feel like her. This presence was different. I went downstairs and there was no smoke, so I turned off the smoke alarm and went back upstairs. Then the alarm went off again. I knew my house wasn't on fire and I thought, *There is someone here.*

I walked downstairs, turned the alarm off again, and I knew that someone was beckoning me into my office. There was the presence of Kerry Packer sitting in my chair. He said, 'Girl, you're going places. Take a seat.' I sat down in front of him on the other side of my desk and he began to give me lessons about the public eye, about media, about how people perceive you and what he expected of me in the public eye. And when Kerry Packer talks to you, you listen – you do not ignore that man.

For three days in my office he gave me verses of wisdom that I wrote down. The first night was from 2am to 6.30am –

it didn't matter to him that I had no sleep. But even though he had a knack of intimidating many people, I was never afraid of him or daunted by his presence – I was just engrossed in his energy. It was almost a sense of relief to know that he had my back (and always has done), and during that time his incredible knowledge and dedication to whatever he's put his mind to just inspired me so much.

Kerry has a very dry sense of humour and during those three days that he taught me, whatever he believed in, he would make sure he got his point across even if I didn't feel we were on the same page at times. I would still listen to everything that he said. This man knew his stuff and knew I was going places and wanted to be part of it. He said, 'The world's not finished with Kerry Packer yet.' And I thought, *Not by a long shot, honey!* Nobody will forget him.

One thing he said to me was, 'I've got no time for idiots and neither have you.' He saw in me a hard working person who goes for what I want and who doesn't expect others to make my way in life. I am fully responsible for where I go in my life. This is why he needed to come in at the beginning to guide me and to make sure I was in control of what happened around me – not allowing others to sidestep me… because I know my stuff, and nobody else can tell me what I know or tell me any different. He told me to stick by my own rules and stay strong.

Those lessons from him have always stuck with me and to this day he still influences me. I feel that he's had a part in me becoming who I am because he saw a lot in me and wanted to help. I feel I have an ongoing connection with Kerry and feel extremely privileged and honoured to have his energy around me. He's still around to inspire me or give me a good kick in the pants when I need it! He's a fascinating man from whom so many can learn so much.

John Lennon

During that time when Kerry Packer was teaching me, he helped me create the Kerry Packer cards – a set of wisdom cards which I'll be releasing in 2015. (Kerry called them the 'Kerry pack o' cards'!). Another person from the spirit world who helped create those cards by inspiring me was former Beatles member and peace activist, John Lennon.

I was sitting watching a TV show and thinking to myself, *What is this world doing to itself? We are killing each other and destroying this planet with the horrendous atrocities that are happening.* Then I felt John Lennon around. He said, 'You can make a difference, you can help change this planet', and I felt this enormous amount of peace.

I want to stress that when these famous people come through, it is not about them and their fame. They come through as normal spirits; it's just that they were famous in this life. With John, it was about him telling me that I need to carry on and help restore peace back to this planet. I could feel his urgency and his enormous emotional pain. I felt John's true calling was his love of peace and this planet.

You might wonder how I knew this was John Lennon. Well, I see the face, I get the name and I just knew who he was. By the time this happened, I was starting to get used to these famous people coming through and I knew that they never wanted me to be overwhelmed because they'd been famous. I wasn't doing backflips because John Lennon was connecting to me; I knew he was there for a reason and I have felt him around many times.

None of these people have come to visit me just for a chat – they are my teachers and I need to sit back and listen. I'm not interested in their celebrity. I respect them but not because they were celebrities. John Lennon was very specific – 'Do whatever it takes to bring peace to people on this planet, even if you do it one by one. You have a gift and you will have the ability so that people will listen to you.'

John talked about war, the innocent lives that had been lost through war and through man's hatred for one another, and the stupid reasons why war was invented. He brought a young man through to me whose name was also John – John K. I was in my office at Minden and I felt John Lennon around and then all of a sudden I felt a young man come through who was an American soldier. John K was a very patriotic young man, very tall, and he told me that he'd wanted to be a soldier from when he was very young. He'd just been killed and had died on the 19th day of the month at 19 years of age. He told me a bit about himself and his love for his family.

John K asked me to look him up and I found a website that had names of people who'd died in the war that month. I couldn't quite get his last name but I knew it started with K. Sure enough there on the website was John K (I won't say his surname) from Philadelphia, 19 years of age, died on 19 April. It was exactly how he'd said it.

I went on to read things about him on Facebook and he was just how I'd felt he was. I was drawn to him and I felt so sad. He had a loving family – his mother, father and two sisters.

He'd been killed only a week or two after going to Afghanistan in his first deployment and it absolutely broke my heart. John K said to me, 'War is wrong.'

I think John Lennon brought John K through to me to show me the devastation. As I was on the website, I scrolled through some of the people who'd been lost in Iraq and Afghanistan and other wars, and I thought about all the wars and all the innocent people who'd been killed. John Lennon also brought through Ted Smout, who was one of the oldest living survivors of WWI. Ted said to me, 'There are no wars overs here. We don't war over here. There is no war against anybody.' He just felt that there was no necessity for war. Ted Smout was a beautiful man and his energy was a strong presence. I only got to meet him once (in spirit) and I was honoured to meet him. These men and women who fight give their lives to give us the free life we have.

I still feel John Lennon and John K around and I feel they're not pushing me but they want me to stop the atrocities against mankind and against animals.

LINDA MCCARTNEY

Linda McCartney, former wife of Beatles member Paul McCartney, came through as a gentle soul but with a very strong presence. A well-known animal activist who created her own range of vegetarian foods that are sold around the world, Linda told me that she'd become vegetarian when she looked at the meat on her plate and realised as she looked out the window at the creatures on her farm that this was what she was eating –

'I'm eating another living, breathing creature who has a life and a soul.' I might add that she didn't say that I should go vegetarian – she understands that it's a matter of personal choice.

Linda is an activist against all the barbaric, inhumane treatment of cattle and sheep and chickens – all of that intensive farming and live exports and abattoir mistreatment – and she asked me to be a part of the campaign to stop the slaughter of whales. She feels that hunting whales is not about animals being used for food to help humans survive and that there are other alternatives instead of killing all of these creatures.

I personally feel that she is an advocate for the animal souls that have been killed for human consumption. She's very passionate about it and wants everyone to at least give it a thought.

So there again, there were lessons for me to learn. Linda McCartney put it into perspective and she always says it's her opinion and doesn't want to force people, but she wants to make sure that people know what's going on. She's upset about the way people disregard where the meat has come from and just wants us to at least think and to give respect to the animals that have died to feed us.

MICHAEL JACKSON

Michael Jackson, one of the best and most famous entertainers ever, actually came through to me as a very humble, down-to-earth person who'd been moulded into the person that someone else wanted him to be. He dearly loved his family.

He said to me, 'We're not celebrities over here. None of us are famous celebrities over here. I can live a normal life without fear of being a celebrity.'

He warned me and said, 'When you become famous, which you will, you need to remember that there are some very strange people out there who'll want to get close to you, who'll want to bring you down, who are jealous of your fame, who will want to stalk you, and who'll tell lies about you. I know that you don't want to become famous – you're not setting out to be that like some people do – but you have to think like a famous person sometimes. You'll end up being in hot water. You'll have to be careful what you say because people are watching you constantly.'

Michael Jackson gave me a lesson for making a transition from someone who can walk down the street unnoticed to someone who can't because the paparazzi are there and they're mobbed – not that I'm saying I'm ever going to be a paparazzi magnet like he was but it's more of a general lesson about dealing with being in the public eye. Up until then I'd never given it a thought, but as Michael explained it to me, it made a lot of sense.

Remember that when they come through, they're not celebrities over there and they're coming through to help me. There are no riches over there. They don't live in mansions and have security guards and so forth.

FREDDIE MERCURY

Who didn't love the lead singer of pop group, Queen? Freddie Mercury was a very flamboyant, interesting man who encouraged me to utilise every single gift that I have. We all know him as a singer, songwriter and musician but he was also apparently a dancer, writer and had a number of different hobbies. He said to me, 'You can sometimes get caught up in things and forget who you are, and sometimes you need to take a step away from the limelight and find yourself again. Always be true to yourself and always be honest with yourself… deeply honest. Ask yourself, "Do you like yourself? Do you like who you've become in all fairness? Do you deserve to be where you are?"'

Freddie talked about a meteorite, the flashing glow of it and how it can strike the ground and you can see it. It strikes the ground with a very small impact but you know it's there – you see this shining light but you don't always see it where it stops. If this meteorite is a massive one it will hit the ground and everyone will know it. I was wondering what he meant by that and he said, 'Some people are stars and they fall to the ground and disappear but some people fall to the ground and make a major impact.' Regarding me, he showed me a massive meteorite which made a huge impact on the planet and he said that that was who I was going to be. He always reminds me to be true to myself and never forget the real me.

HEATH LEDGER

Heath Ledger was of course a very talented young Aussie actor whose many fans were shattered when he died.

One day I found myself lying in bed with him! Let me explain… he was on one side of the bed and I was on the other (in the other realm, not physically). Nothing was going on of course – there was no physical contact as we were just sitting up in bed. Suddenly, I broke wind very loudly and I just burst out laughing and he looked at me and went, 'You dirty cow!' And we both started laughing.

We were talking for awhile like old mates and he said, 'You've got to remember to laugh. You've got to remember to have some fun.' I was laughing the whole time because of the way he was talking to me. I felt embarrassed at breaking the wind but he didn't feel embarrassed and he wanted me to remember to make fun of myself sometimes. I could see where he was coming from because it was extremely embarrassing to me, but he thought it was hilarious, and in his own way he was saying to me not to be too hard on myself and to laugh at myself.

I just loved his sense of humour and his very down-to-earth manner. He said, 'Never be over-sensitive about yourself. Take the good with the bad. People will criticise you and try to bring you down, and when you feel that way, remember… you farted in bed with Heath Ledger!' He took things so personally and was so sensitive when he was alive, and he wanted to make sure I knew that I shouldn't be sensitive about what people said and thought about me. He wanted me to know that I should just let it go. (I have a funny feeling that this story will be the one I'm always going to be asked about by journalists!)

BON SCOTT

The original AC/DC frontman, Bon Scott, was extremely cheeky and rather crude but had a heart of gold. He was a very misunderstood and very talented man who, like me, also knew from a young age that he was going to be famous. He said, 'In this industry, from what I learnt there are many lecherous sharks who will try and get every dollar and cent out of you with total disregard for your talents and who you are. The greedy, selfish money-hungry sharks are everywhere.'

He showed me a picture of me in the ocean with these great white sharks circling me, and he said, 'I was a victim of many of these circling sharks who would take a chunk out of me, but I would still live. One would take a leg, I would still live. One would take an arm, I would still live. They will take chunks out of you and you need to be aware of these people who are so full of greed and don't care about the person you are. All they see are dollar signs.'

Bon Scott warned me, 'Don't trust anyone; only trust yourself. It can turn friends against friends and family against family, and it can consume you so that you become bitter and angry because people stole off you and you were broke and down to your last dollar and the producers have taken everything.' Bon said, 'I can never let that happen to you.' So he puts a watchful eye over me, and I've been aware of him telling me not to take a particular deal – he'll say no.

When these amazing souls are around they will usually give me signs that the information I have received is indeed from them. Bon was talking to me about signing a contract – making sure I always read what was in it, getting someone else to read it and making sure I knew exactly what I was signing. A couple of days after this chat with Bon, I was at the shops and the lady in front of me was wearing an AC/DC t-shirt. I started to laugh as Bon was looking straight at me on the back of this shirt. I said to the lady, 'I love that t-shirt', and she replied 'Yes! I haven't worn it for years but I found it in the back of the cupboard when I was clearing things out and I just felt I wanted to wear it today, I don't know why.' I laughed to myself and thought, *I know exactly why you needed to wear it today. Bon, you cheeky devil as you always are... LOL!*

AC/DC always knew they were good and were destined for fame but as he said, there were a lot of 'thieving bastards' out there. He also seems to be a guardian of men around me now that I'm alone since Mick passed, like a big brother watching over me. He'll say, 'You're not good enough.' 'You're not her type.' 'You're definitely a prick.'! With single men that I've come in contact with, it feels to me that Bon will let me know who the right guy is in good time. He's a very deep, caring person under all those tattoos and everything else.

MICHAEL HUTCHENCE

The first time I spoke to the late, great INXS frontman, Michael Hutchence, was because his lawyer had organised a reading. He had been a friend of Michael's for a long time and it was a personal reading, so for reasons of confidentiality there is only so much I can divulge and Michael will only allow me to say so much out of respect for his family. When I started the reading, I didn't even know it was Michael Hutchence because when famous people come through, they don't tell me who they are and I don't want to know anything beforehand – if they're famous I don't want to know that.

Michael Hutchence came through and talked briefly about his passing but nothing in-depth, and the person on the other end of the phone who I was doing the reading for knew that it was him. Michael talked about his daughter and what he wanted for her in life and he also talked about the relationship he had with Paula Yates and the musical talents of his lawyer, which included opera and other pursuits. He talked about the last few years of his life which I won't talk anymore about, but what I can tell you, is that he was a compassionate, loving family man who got a little bit caught up in fame but thoroughly enjoyed the ride.

Michael's early passing was heartbreaking to so many and he's sorry to all his fans that in the prime of his life and career, he left this planet. He wants to thank all his fans and the people who loved him right from the beginning when INXS started. They are all appreciated for their adoration and trust in him. Once, I had just had a lesson from Michael and I was driving along and the song, *The Gift*, by INXS came on. I started to laugh as I knew it was from him.

STEVE IRWIN

I'll talk much more about Steve Irwin and his profound impact on me and my life in the Animal Communications section but what I'll say now is that Steve seems to be preparing me for the limelight. He said to me, 'Mate, don't react to the rubbish and the criticism people are going to throw at you. Never let it get to you what people say.' He told me that I'll be put under the microscope but to just be true to myself and be who I truly am, and that he will help me make it through. He said, 'Focus on what you are meant to be doing and just forge ahead with your goals and the real reason you are here.'

SHIRLEY STRACHAN

Graeme 'Shirley' Strachan was the lead singer of successful 1970s Australian pop group, Skyhooks, who also went on to become a much loved TV personality. Sadly, he was killed in a helicopter accident. He first came through to family members in a reading, and I was unaware that he was someone famous until the end of the reading, just like with Michael Hutchence. He has since come through and said to me, 'Be who you want to be. Be who you are. Let no man tell you who you should be. Nobody told me who I had to be. If you didn't like who I was, then that was your problem, not mine.' He told me to stay strong and be true to myself and said that there are a lot of people out there trying to tell you who to be, especially in this industry. Both Shirley and Michael were very strong in telling me that.

JOHN DENVER

John Denver was of course a huge singing superstar and he was also a great advocate for environmentalism. I have felt him around a number of times when there have been environmental issues coming up. I've felt him being very active there and helping me by giving me advice.

I feel that John Denver, like the rest of these famous people, has his place in helping me along the way. He very much cared for the area that he lived in and kept talking to me about the wilderness in Aspen. Everyone knows that he had a hit single with *Rocky Mountain High* but I didn't realise that he actually had a home in the Rocky Mountains in Aspen, Colorado. I started feeling him around and I felt that as I was starting to become more involved in environmental causes that John Denver wants to be a part of that. I feel that he will make his presence more and more known as I progress with this.

Not long after I connected to John, I met up with a friend of mine who hadn't known that I'd connected to him, and my friend said, 'Oh by the way, look at this jacket. It used to belong to John Denver. I bought it in an auction and I've got the certificate of authenticity and a photo of John Denver wearing it.' And I just stood there with my eyes wide open and thought, *Well, that's validation, isn't it!* My friend asked me if the jacket had been John Denver's, and when I felt the jacket I definitely felt John's very peaceful, environment-loving energy. I said to my friend, 'You've definitely got John Denver's jacket.'

Brian Connolly

Brian Connolly was the lead singer for popular '70s English band, Sweet. He has talked to me about personal safety and making sure I'm always safe wherever I go. I sometimes travel alone but always feel safe as he watches over me. He told me to never underestimate fans and the lengths they will go to just to be near me and that I always need to be conscious of that. He wasn't trying to scare me and said that most of the time I will be fine, but to just always be aware of my safety, which I am.

JADE GOODY

This one was a surprise! Jade Goody's name will be very familiar to people living in the U.K. and probably not so well known in Australia and other countries. She was an English celebrity who first made her name in the British version of the reality TV show, *Big Brother*, and who was diagnosed with cervical cancer. She passed away at just 28 years of age. I'd seen something about Jade on TV and felt an instantaneous connection to her. I thought to myself, *She's passed over but she's so young*, and then it said on the show that she had indeed passed away even though I hadn't known. She had the cancer and ignored it and it had gone through her system. She seems very much to be an advocate of people listening to their own bodies and not ignoring any signs.

When she came through to me she said, 'Before engaging your big fat trap and getting into all kinds of trouble, think about what you say.' She had been controversial in *Big Brother* because of some of the things she'd said so she'd had experience with the subject. Jade also told me, 'I like the simplicity of life and I'd come from near-poverty and a council house background, but then all of a sudden I came into this money.' She said to invest wisely because after time you're not going to want to be in the limelight, so when you get that money just think about what you want to do with it. I had been thinking about that beforehand – that I want to give to charity and help people. She talked about greed and selfishness in people and said that she knew I wasn't like that. She said, 'You will help charities and help people. You will have an abundance of money.'

I'll point out here that money has never been an issue with me. I want enough to buy my house and to live comfortably and with the rest I want to help others, and Jade will be there to show me – to put charities in front of me – so I know that something needs a hand. Because she says, 'You could not possibly spend all the money that you have. How big a house do you need?' She knows that my needs are not lavish and over the top. I live simply. I don't need an expensive car or a mansion.

She also said, 'Stay true to yourself financially. Make sure your house is safe and there is security. Your home should be your fortress. My home was continually bombarded. Be careful about what you say with your family, with politics, with religion and your personal financial situation. Don't tell anybody; they don't need to know.' She made the mistake of telling everyone that she had a considerable amount of money in the bank and people came out of the woodwork with their hand out. She told me to beware of the family and people you haven't seen in over 20 years who suddenly appear. She knew she was going to die and had to make sure that her young boys were going to be alright.

Jade also talked to me about my healing abilities and how very profound they are, and that she sees the healing abilities in me as extremely powerful. She tells me that in the future a lot of people will want to connect because of my abilities, so she's warning me to be careful because I can't help everybody all the time. She thinks people may want to break in and physically touch me. She knew what that was like, with people wanting to be near her and touch her, jumping the fence and stealing her clothes off her clothesline and such.

I have come to realise recently that what Jade said about my healing abilities is starting to come true and it has been quite profound how I've healed some people of long-held ailments that doctors haven't been able to help. One man, who'd had back pain for 20 years and who'd spent thousands of dollars and seen many different doctors, still had no change. He came to me for a reading and I picked up via body talk that he needed a healing. Within three days he had no back pain! I have had quite a lot of very positive feedback from my healings.

LESSONS FROM THE FAMOUS

All these famous people with their experiences have been able to coach me to be who I decide to be and who I truly feel I am inside. They have helped me in so many ways. It seems like these profound people don't so much want their name out there and to still be famous but they want to be a part of where I'm going, because their name could help me succeed in what they want to see happen to this planet.

They can see a lot more over there (in the afterlife) than what we can over here – the impending damage and the way we are destroying the planet. They want us to know:

Change your ways. Change your habits. Change your thoughts.

These many beautiful celebrity souls seem to have come through with this mantra, if you'd like to call it that. If we change our ways, our habits and our thoughts, then the earth will be a better place. As it stands now, we are killing it and there will be nothing left for future generations. These people want to get this out there – it's kind of like when Michael Jackson got the celebrities together to record *We Are the World.* They're doing their own little Michael Jackson get-together in the afterlife to help me get it out there and help stop the destruction of this planet, because as far as I can see there is no other planet out there like this – not that we can get to anyway. And as they say, we don't deserve another planet. It's like buying a brand new car and totalling it. Once it's written off, it's written off – that's it. That's what they're showing me.

These famous people teach me patience and make me wait until they feel I am ready for the next stage in my lessons. I listen intently to everything every one of these powerful souls says and to the words of wisdom that they've given me over the years as they've all been through it themselves.

I have always felt comfortable and very comforted from the moment I knew these souls were there, knowing these amazing souls who once were very powerful people on this planet are now very much a part of my journey. I am not the only one these souls help, as they are not all just for me – they do help others in a similar journey to me but only a chosen few as far as I know, and they all have their own people that they're meant to help. I continue to communicate with most of my celebrity friends who have passed over – it's never a one-off thing. As I become more and more well known, I feel them around for one reason or another and always feel that comfort to know they have my back.

While I've been talking to my editor in her suburban Brisbane lounge room about all of this, it's occurred to me that nowhere in the world has there been such a gathering of powerful souls all coming together to have their say and telling all of you reading this book about their part in helping me, in their own words and one by one through their connection to me. The information I've received is all in their own words directly from them all individually.

ANIMAL COMMUNICATIONS

*A*nyone who knows me will know that I'm at least as well known, if not more well known, for my psychic connections with animals as for my connections to people. I can safely say that there aren't many people in this world who can connect to people who've passed over and to animals that have passed or that are still alive. This part of my gift can of course be witnessed each week in the *Woman's Day* magazine where my 'Animal Whisperer' column appears, and as you can see if you read it, the people I do the readings for give feedback on how accurate my readings are – I'm usually pretty spot on.

STEVE AND TERRI IRWIN

A big part of my journey with animals was the legendary 'Crocodile Hunter', the late, great Steve Irwin who as I've told you,

I had the honour of working with at the Queensland Reptile and Fauna Park. As I'm writing this, Steve has just said, 'Keep it brief and not too long-winded', so his lesson to me is, 'Don't blah blah blah on forever. Keep to the point.' That sounds like Steve!

How would you describe a man who has such deep passion for the planet and for the animals who inhabit it? He loved all creatures and natural things, from the tiniest little ant to the biggest redwood tree in California. Steve used to say that he and Terri were so different but so very alike – their difference of views on business and so forth. Terri was always the powerhouse behind the business whereas Steve really had no interest in the business, but Terri had the compassion for the animals that Steve did. Their meeting was no accident and their union was no accident.

THE QUEENSLAND REPTILE AND FAUNA PARK

I first met Steve and Terri just before *The Crocodile Hunter* TV show was released. A not-so-famous Steve's favourite saying to me was, 'How's your bum for grubs?' I thought it was a little crass but that was just Steve! I got to know him when Terri offered me a job at the Queensland Reptile and Fauna Park, a quiet little boutique establishment, not well visited, but enough to make ends meet. That was about to change, of course. Steve became a huge, worldwide star and the park morphed into the now famous Australia Zoo.

Over morning teas with Steve and Terri and the staff of seven people – sometimes Steve's parents, Bob and Lyn, would be there –

we would sit down and have a good laugh. Steve would come into what was then a very small café, and next to it was the old entrance with the souvenir shop. He would laugh at the souvenirs – the little crocodile pencil sharpeners and such – and I remember Terri had ordered these crocodile hats with the jaws of the crocodile coming out above your head. Steve thought this was hilarious. He made us all wear one, which was typical of Steve, but underneath that fun-loving side, you could see a man who had absolute respect and compassion for the animals, for the earth, and for Terri. These two were chalk and cheese but were also on the same wavelength, and being with them you could see the deep love and incredibly powerful connection they had for each other and always will do.

One day Steve came in for his morning toasty – he always had a toasted chicken, cheese and onion sandwich for morning tea – and I was putting some ice-blocks into the freezer. It was a big chest freezer and I was leaning right over into it. Next minute Steve grabbed me by the ankles and upended me straight into it, so all you could see was this pair of legs dangling out of the freezer! I was cursing and laughing because I knew darn well it was him. He loved to play jokes on people.

I also remember when I worked there that Steve's dog, Suey, was very much a part of things. She was an amazing, incredibly intelligent dog and she loved me. If I had to go somewhere in the ute, she would appear out of nowhere and jump in that ute with me and off we'd go. She never did it with anyone else, only me, and I knew that she was talking to me. She'd say, 'I like you, you're really nice!'

I connected with all of those animals and Steve and Terri gave me a lot of responsibility, like looking after Harriet, the Galapagos land tortoise. She was a huge star and I'd go to her every morning and say, 'What would you like to eat, darling?' and she would say something like, 'You know that pawpaw stuff you gave me yesterday? That was really nice.'

Amanda with Harriet, the Galapagos land tortoise

One day I'd picked up a very large rhino iguana from the airport on the way home and taken it out to my place where it stayed in my laundry overnight. I looked at it and it said, 'What do you think you're doing? Are you going to let me out or what?' But I thought it would be alright and it stayed there the night until I took it to the park the next morning.

It was a small park and I had a special connection with all of those animals, including Amelia, the wedge tailed eagle who was hit by a semitrailer. Terri and I had to carry her in this massive box joined by a pole. Those talons would rip you apart but Amelia allowed me to look at her and see how much damage was done. I nursed her back to health and she was released back to the wild – something Terri was a big advocate of us doing as much as we possibly could. You could see how much the animals loved her too and every single one of those animals loved me and I loved them. I just felt so at home with the animals with their unconditional love. I knew that they were happy even though they were in captivity. They didn't feel trapped, not one of them. And they all loved Steve and Terri.

Animals are so intuitive and I can also feel when they're not keen on someone. There was one guy there called John who wasn't a very nice character. None of the people liked him – he was a nasty, negative person – and you could tell the animals didn't like him either. He caused a lot of trouble with the staff and he wasn't really compassionate for the animals even though he was basically one of the bosses of the park at the time.

All in all, it was an amazing time and very much a time of learning for me, with these incredibly beautiful and unique creatures of this planet that most people in their everyday lives would never have the opportunity to work with.

NURTURING MY ANIMAL COMMUNICATIONS

While I was at the Queensland Reptile and Fauna Park, Steve taught me a lot about animals and I guess he was the one who really brought the animal communicator out in me. I would do croc talks and snake talks and I would feed the 10-metre long reticulated pythons, saltwater crocodiles, snakes, lizards and spiders. Some of these creatures could kill someone in a few seconds but Steve taught me to never be fearful of them, and even though I would work with the most dangerous, I was never fearful. I learnt to respect and love them for each species that they are and for where they belong on earth.

I learnt so much from Steve and from Terri, and still to this day Steve and his compassion for this planet and for those animals is with me. He still comes through and advises me on animals – not about the telepathic communications with them – and I've spoken with him on many occasions since he's passed.

STEVE PASSING OVER

Because I knew Steve, he came to me not long after he passed, and his words were, 'I haven't left ya, mate.' On the day that he passed – I remember it well – I had this feeling of dread again. Mick and I had had breakfast on the balcony and he said, 'What's the matter, Chubb? You're down about something.' And I said, 'I don't know, there's a real feeling of dread, of loss.' I went and had a shower and felt Eric around and he said, 'Remember how you felt when I passed? Remember that feeling of loss?' And I said, 'Yes, that was so painful,' and for some reason Eric and my Guides wanted me to remember the pain that I felt.

I told Mick I was taking the kids shopping, then when I was pushing the trolley around the shopping centre, all these people were crying. I said, 'What's going on?' Someone said, 'Steve Irwin's just died.' It was like my whole soul just became so incredibly sad. The whole world was mourning, and I thought instantaneously, *Terri*. I made contact with the park, Terri wasn't there but I spoke to her personal assistant.

I was living up at Eumundi when Steve died and I had film crews at my house afterwards and they were ringing me – somehow they found out my phone number – because they knew that I knew Steve and Terri and also what I now do for a living. They wanted to know, 'Have you spoken to Steve? Has he come through?' Mick said to me, 'It's a bloody circus out there, Chubb.' He was answering the phone and going out and saying to the journalists, 'Mate, get lost and leave us alone.' Remember, he was six foot six and 137 kilos so when he told you to get off his property, you went... and they did!

COMMUNICATIONS WITH STEVE SINCE HIS PASSING

Bob Irwin (Steve's father), who's still very active in conservation, came to me because he wanted to talk to Steve and also to his wife, Lyn, who was lost in an accident a year before Steve passed. He's spoken to them both and Bob and I have become good friends. I have an incredible respect for him and what he believes in, and you could tell the love and respect that Steve has and always will have for his father.

When Steve comes to me since he's passed over, his sense of humour is intact. What you saw with Steve was what he was, that sometimes over-the-top character. That was who he was – that was no put-on – but there was always another side to him. If you hurt his animals, you'd know about it. He'd be like, 'You hurt any animal and I'll make sure you suffer for it.' He talked about the whaling and I asked if he wanted me to be a part of it and go on the boat that tries to stop it (The Sea Shepherd). But he said, 'No, it's too dangerous.'

He also talked about the Malaysian orang-utan and the destruction of the Amazon rainforest, the lungs of this planet, and how hard it has hit him even though he has passed over. He still feels incredible emotional pain for this planet. He's got no time for people who are greedy and selfish and who perform or direct others to 'disembowel' (as he puts it) this planet. But he has time for people like myself and the people who are trying to stop the destruction and the carnage of the earth and its animals.

I was so fortunate to work with Steve and Terri Irwin and those marvellous creatures at the Reptile Park. Both Bob Irwin and Terri own large tracts of land now that are to be preserved for wilderness and that are never to be built on – a very special legacy for the Irwin family. My mother and Steve are really great mates on the other side and they are always joking with each other and having a laugh. Mum absolutely loves Steve and he loves her even though they never met in this life.

HEALING

From a very young age, I sensed a feeling of being able to heal and I believe it is going to figure more and more in my life and work. I remember being about seven years of age on my uncle's farm in Mayfield in England. My cousin, Cherry (now deceased), had a cat that had been injured by a vehicle. It had quite severe injuries and by the time I went back to the farm, the cat had been injured for about three weeks. It had seen a local vet but wasn't in good shape at all.

The cat had a major limp and I knew that it had hurt its back left leg and that there were internal injuries as well as in the left eye. I remember picking the cat up and all of a sudden I felt a blue, very powerful healing light come through me into my hands. I brought the cat to my chest and held it there for probably about half an hour, bringing a healing through. I could sense that the cat was very open to this and had felt very comfortable, and I felt the cat saying, 'This feels wonderful. I'm feeling so much better.'

Two or three times a day I would hold her to me, and after about the third day she would come looking for me for her healing treatment, which amazed everyone as she was not a very social cat with anyone. Over the course of the week that I was there at the farm, I saw this cat improve every single day. I knew that she was recovering at a rapid pace. I had been giving her daily healing treatments and by the time I left a week later, she wasn't even limping. I knew that she was making a full recovery because of what I'd done. I then somehow knew how to do distant healing on her – meaning that I wasn't anywhere near her physically but could still send the healing energy to her – and I also knew it was working

Apparently after that healing, she would go and sleep on the bed that I'd slept in while I was visiting the farm. For a cat that was not even supposed to survive, she lived on for another eight years.

Since then I've done many successful healings on people and animals with many different ailments. Recently a lady rang me about her quite unwell farm dog. This dog had very little mobility but was still only young. I continued a healing session for two days, connecting to the dog regularly, and after three days the dog was jumping in and out of the back of the ute.

Another recent healing was a friend of mine's husband who is a very keen golf player and who was unable to play for three weeks because of a shoulder injury. I did a two-day healing session and after the third day he was back out on the golf course – 'in full swing', as he put it. He was ever so grateful – he loves his golf!

These two recent events were both distant healings as they were both in different states from where I live. Many people find it fascinating that I can do my readings and healings from long distances away, but as my many satisfied clients know, my readings and healings are just as accurate and effective by phone or by email as they are when I'm in the same room with someone.

How this works is, my healing Guides know exactly where that healing energy needs to go anywhere on this planet. I have what's known as an 'intention', and that intention is to send through my healing Guides a healing energy directly to that person or to that animal. In other words, I intend to heal the person or animal with the ailments. My healing Guides are well aware of my request for the type of healing for this person or animal, and the healing energy is sent directly to that person or animal. I know this gift is very powerful and I have helped many people and pets, including one cat that had severe renal problems. He is now fit and healthy and living a life he always wanted on his mum and dad's farm.

I feel so blessed and privileged to be able to use this gift for so many good intentions and to be able to take pain away from people and animals. It creates a much happier and more productive life for that person or that pet.

Over the years I have tweaked and worked the healing process and now I have a very strong understanding of the whole method. Each healing for each person or animal is unique and tailored to that specific person – no two healings are the same. First, I do 'body talk' – I get the feeling from their body of what is wrong with them and work out where this illness came from and what caused it to turn into a physical ailment. Then I deal with both the emotional and physical, clearing blocked energies and allowing the body to heal itself. The person or pet receiving the healing doesn't need to do a thing as I set in place the healing process for however long it may take. For example, it may be an injury of some kind and I will know how long I need to work on a person or pet on a daily basis.

The longest I've had to work on someone was eight weeks. This lady, who'd just had a breast removal operation because of cancer, had heard about me and contacted me. As far as I know from her reports back to me, she got through the chemotherapy very well. She did lose some of her hair but overall her energy was much better than she expected and her overall emotional state was also very positive.

My grandfather, Walter, has a lot to do with the healing side of things as he was an ambulance officer in the war and worked in a hospital. Also, my mum and both her sisters were nurses so there's a strong line through the family for healing. I'd like to point out here that my healings never intrude on the western treatments being prescribed, whether they are medications or treatment such as chemotherapy – my healings work *with* them, not against them.

I am what is known as a Pranic Healer. I now have many healing certificates to my name, and Pranic Healing is one that I was drawn to most. It is the process of using the energies from the universe to get the bodies to heal themselves with a little bit of help from me and my healing Guides.

READINGS

When I'm conducting a reading, I am given no prior information regarding the person or pet having the reading, nor am I told anything except what type of a reading this person wants and their first name. I prefer to have no information as I want to hear validation from the loved ones who have passed. People ask how I could possibly get information for them over the phone if we are thousands of miles apart. The answer is that I receive the information directly from their Guides and loved ones telepathically and give the information I receive to them.

Every reading is different, whether it's 10,000 miles away over the phone or face to face. The people or animals I connect with always know what clients want the reading to be about and from which loved ones they want to hear. Sometimes clients have questions they want to ask, but usually by the time we've finished the reading and they look at the questions, they have all been answered. Sometimes the passed-over souls are unable to answer certain questions, not because they don't know the answer, but because it is our journey to find out the answer ourselves.

MESSAGES AND VALIDATIONS

It's very important for people having readings to receive validation so this is why their passed-over loved ones and pets tell me specific things that I couldn't possibly know. Very often no-one else knows them either because they're so personal. An example of validation happened when a lady in Scotland was having a reading over the phone and her beautiful husband came through. He told her he knew she had his folded up handkerchief with some of his hair in it under her pillow, and she slept with that every night. Nobody else knew that except her. So I ask the loved ones for specifics, please, and I treat everybody with the utmost respect. Many come through from the afterlife and thank me very much for passing on the messages to their loved ones, and it really helps the loved ones passed over to feel peace and closure too.

People are often comforted to know that our passed-over loved ones always know what is going on in our lives. They will go to weddings, engagements, birthday parties and anything else of celebration that's happening in their family. They've often been known to frequent grandchildren's football games or sporting events – I often hear them in the background yelling and screaming at the games! – and they get just as excited as we do and still love to be a part of our lives.

Sometimes they come to me specifically to ask me to pass on a message to their loved ones here. One example was a client of mine who lives in another state – her son came to me independently and I knew exactly who his mother was. The son said, 'Please pass this message on to my mum. I know my sister is marrying my best friend from childhood next weekend.' I rang this lady and gave her the message and she was shocked, as indeed her daughter was marrying her son's childhood best friend. He also laughed at his mum and said, 'I'm not real sure about the red hair, Mum.' She told me that she had just had her hair dyed the day before – from brown to red! This message gave the family so much peace before this happy event.

Sometimes strange and fascinating things happen when I'm conducting a reading. I was in my office doing a face-to-face reading for one lady and her father came through. Apparently, as he told me, he lived with her the last five years of his life and he would leave all the doors open, which would annoy her. Suddenly, my office door flung open and the lady and I looked at each other and we both started to laugh. There was no breeze in the house nor was there any ability for this door to fling open by itself the way it did. So she knew that it was her father.

Another time I was on the Sunshine Coast doing some readings from an event room. My car was parked right outside the room and it had been locked all day. A lady came to see me for a reading and her father told her he was the one who was placing the feathers that she'd been finding in the strangest of places. Later on, I'd just finished for the day and I had still felt this lovely man around. I got into my car and there was a good-sized feather on the console of my car! I knew it hadn't been there that morning and that no-one had been in the car all day, and my car at the time was a BMW with a very good alarm system, so no-one had broken into it. This lovely man laughed and said he'd put the feather in my car to thank me for the wonderful reading I'd given him and his daughter. I still have the feather to this day.

Sometimes the passed-over souls know the questions that we're going to ask them during our connection with them. One lady's son who had passed from an accident knew his mother wanted to know that she had now done some improvements and changed his room around to her own craft room. The first thing he said to his mother was, 'The room looks great, and you are welcome to use it as your craft room.' This was her validation.

One lady having her first reading was very nervous. I brought through her daughter who'd been killed suddenly in an accident. She laughed at her mother's recent attempt to clear out the Tupperware cupboard and match up the lids to the containers. The mother and daughter both thought this was hilarious as this event had only occurred the day before. These two then went on to have a beautiful connection. The lady was the only one home that day and no-one else knew she'd sorted out the Tupperware cupboard. This was the daughter's validation to let her mum know that she was with her.

Sometimes they just know things before we do, as in the case of one lady whose son came through and told her that her sister – his aunty – was finally pregnant, and that she was going to have a little girl. The lady was unaware of this, but a few days later she emailed my office to tell me that her sister, after trying for five years to conceive, was indeed now pregnant. I then got another email a few months later to say that she was having a girl. Another email a few months after that told me of the arrival of a healthy baby girl.

TWO UNEXPECTED COMMUNICATIONS

Just when I thought I'd completed this book, two unexpected communications came through to me when I was appearing at the Pet Expo at the Gold Coast in October, 2014. They were both so powerful that I had to include them here.

Here I was at the Pet Expo thinking it was going to be a lovely day just connecting to all the gorgeous pets and getting lots of doggy kisses, but I also had a feeling that something big was about to happen. I'd been smelling smoke around my home for about two weeks to the point where I thought my house might've been on fire. There were two different types of smoke smells – one was chemical and the other was like burning wood.

Anyway, two ladies who were sisters came to me for a private reading before my public appearance, and I brought through their pets, both living and passed over, and then I connected to a lady who told me she'd just recently passed over in the past couple of months. The ladies both took deep breaths and looked at me very intensely. I said that this lady had known them both for a very long time and that she always loved to give them wet, sloppy kisses on the cheek. I then told them she knew that the new building they were now in for work was having a lot of air-conditioning problems even though it was a brand new building. She also mentioned the no-sugar morning teas in the staffroom and that she was the one who was playing around with the TV, switching it on and off while meetings were going on.

The lady then mentioned that she was now with her partner who'd passed over about two years earlier from cancer.

She also showed me that her passing was very quick and that she did not suffer in any way. I saw her sitting in a passenger seat and she was moving very fast. I suddenly saw a flash of light, and for obvious reasons I'm not going to go into detail, but she showed me what happened next and I knew then that this was the MH17 plane that had been shot down over the Ukraine on 17 July, 2014. It was during this time that I again smelt that chemical smoke. I then felt all of the other passengers coming through, letting me know they were all there. And let me tell you, they did not suffer. It was so quick – a massive explosion.

I was just shocked to my core and the two ladies and I cried and hugged each other. I was a mess and had to go on stage in about five minutes so I composed myself and professionally went out to connect to people's pets in the audience. But I had to take some time out for myself to get my thoughts together, as you can imagine. I was very emotional, witnessing what I saw in great detail, but Spirit realised that I was strong enough to deal with it or they would not have shown me. I was an emotional mess, and less than two hours later more was to come.

After I did the public show I had a few more private readings booked, and a lady came in for a pet connection. It started off as normal with me connecting to her animals, both passed over and living, and then I suddenly saw two people and their two dogs that had passed come through. These people told me that this lady had lived in the area for many years and that they and many others were her friends and neighbours. I then smelt the burning wood type of smoke and I said that these two people and their dogs had perished in a bushfire.

It turned out that this lady lost these people and animals in the Black Saturday fires on 7 February, 2009, in Victoria – the worst bushfires in Australia's recorded history.

I then saw many other people coming through with their pets that had also passed in the fire. I also saw many other animals – both domestic and wildlife – that had been taken by this devastating bushfire. Again, as with the MH17 communications, there were so many souls wanting me to know they were there. Many were pets trying to let their owners know they knew their owners loved them and that many were trying to get back to their homes to save their much loved pets. Again, I saw in detail what had happened to these people and animals, and thank goodness it was very quick for them. In the terrible tragedy, 173 people lost their lives and it broke my heart to see all the pets and wildlife that also lost their lives on this terrible day in Australian history.

That night after the expo, I was absolutely emotionally exhausted and went back to my unit where I was staying near the beach. I cancelled my plans for that night and sat down to watch some TV. What are the odds of being on the Gold Coast and also at the Pet Expo and these two very different tragedies come through – one being from the Ukraine and the other from Victoria, Australia? As I sat down that Saturday night to unwind and relax, the first show that came on the moment I'd switched on the TV had a title with the same first name as the lady who'd passed on the MH17 flight. So that was her sign to let me know that I did indeed connect to her.

These two amazing and emotionally difficult connections were confirmed to be true, both from the friends of that lady who confirmed everything else that I'd said about her, and also the lady with the Black Saturday connections. I certainly did not ask for either of these things to come to me and I didn't expect them, but when they do come, all I can do is bring these souls through to say what they want and need to say.

WARNINGS

Sometimes warnings are given in readings, as happened for one lady when her father came through. He told her, 'This Christmas coming up keep my grandson out of the red Commodore.' He repeated this several times with a sense of urgency. She said, 'He doesn't know anyone, as far as I know, who drives a red Commodore.' But she did pass the warnings on to her son, especially around Christmas time. At Christmas time the young man was at a party and a friend of his had just turned up in a red Holden Commodore. The young man was going to get into the passenger side of the car and realised what his grandfather had said. His gut feeling screamed, 'Don't get in!' He got out and five minutes later this vehicle was wrapped around a lamp post, killing the passenger. His mother was so grateful she sent me a week's holiday, all expenses paid, as I saved her only son's life. Sadly, someone else had lost their son that day.

These warnings can sometimes take years to make their presence known, as one lady found out. Her brother came through and told her that the new shed and the extension on her home which had just recently been erected had not been cleared by the builder to the council. Her brother mentioned it several times and told her to get it sorted, which she never did, thinking that the builder had it under control. Five years later they went to sell the house and found out that the extension and the shed had not been council-approved. She rang to tell me that she is now kicking herself because they had to pull the shed down and the extension was illegal.

IMPATIENT SOULS

You might not think that people who have passed over can be impatient or excited but it can happen. Sometimes they'll get there early and just sit and wait for their turn when I'm doing readings. One gentleman who was passed over turned up in my office at 8am and his loved one's reading was at 9.30am. I knew who he wanted to connect to and I was quite happy for him to sit and wait. When his daughter called at 9.30am for her reading, I laughed and said, 'Your father has been here since 8am sitting quietly and waiting.' She laughed and told me that no matter where he was going or what he was doing, he was always early. Hilarious! He said that he had visited her that morning and chuckled that she'd had cheesecake for breakfast. She was a bit surprised at her father knowing her unusual breakfast choice as indeed she had eaten cheesecake for breakfast. Apparently, cheesecake had been his favourite food too.

Another reading was a lovely man passed over who turned up with some golf clubs. He was waiting for his brother to have his reading later on that day. When his brother arrived, I told him that his passed-over brother had been waiting for the past hour or so and had been sitting there with some golf clubs. When I started the reading, the golf clubs then came up again and the brother passed said, 'I know you have my golf clubs in the boot of your car and you are welcome to them.' Indeed, the brother took me out and showed me his passed-over brother's very expensive golf clubs in the back of the car. He uses them on a regular basis.

It does not take people long after passing to get messages to loved ones, as in the case of a Mt. Isa couple. This couple received a phone call while they were crossing the road to have a scheduled reading with me. The phone call was to tell them that the man's uncle had just passed away only a couple of hours before. Fifteen minutes after the phone call, the couple were sitting in front of me when the uncle who'd only just passed made his presence known. He told me that he had just passed and sent his love to his family. He wanted them to know that he knew he was much loved. He also told me that he'd just passed from cancer and had arrived safely on the other side. The couple were so shocked about this as you can imagine, receiving a phone call about this passing just 15 minutes earlier.

UNEXPECTED MESSAGES

Sometimes we never know who's going to turn up from the afterlife to get a message to their loved ones, as was the case with a lady in Ireland. The lovely lady had called me for her reading and I'd brought her family through. Towards the end of the reading, a young boy came through saying his mother's name was Marion and his name was Peter and he had drowned when he was seven nearly 50 years before.

As this lady was fairly new to the area, she did not know many of the neighbours. She began to ask a few people if they knew Marion, who in actual fact lived seven houses up from her. When she dug a little deeper, she found out that indeed Marion had a son called Peter who drowned at the age of seven nearly 50 years earlier. When the lady's recorded CD of her reading arrived (which I always send to my clients), she then played it to Marion who was so shocked but absolutely thrilled to hear the messages from her much loved son.

Sometimes passed-over people just turn up to connect to their loved ones that I may be crossing paths with on that day. One day I was in getting my passport and I sat beside a lady. I suddenly felt a mother figure around her asking me if she could please talk to her daughter sitting beside me. I was happy to bring through a message but wondered how I was going to approach this stranger sitting beside me. I turned to her and said, 'Excuse me, has your mother passed?' The lady looked quite bewildered and said, 'Yes.' I then said to her, 'Your mother is a little upset at your sister about the will.' The lady was very shocked at what her mother knew about what was going on in the family regarding her house and her will. So I brought through her mother for about ten minutes which in turn brought her a lifetime of peace. I think she was just so shocked at the validation and the in-depth information I knew that she did not question my authenticity.

Another lovely lady sat beside me in a plane from Brisbane to Melbourne. Even before the plane took off, I suddenly heard a man singing *When the Saints Go Marching In*. I knew he was connected to the elderly lady sitting beside me. He sang through taxiing down the runway, taking off, and in mid-air!

I had to bring him through as he was relentless. I turned to the lady and said, 'I am a medium and your husband is coming through.' She sat quietly and nodded her head. He told me his name was Bob and I told her, 'He keeps continuously singing *When the Saints Go Marching In*.' She looked at me in utter shock and told me Bob was her husband. He told her on his deathbed that if he could get a message to her that he was okay, he would sing his favourite football anthem. He had been a diehard supporter of the Saints for many years (the Melbourne AFL team, St. Kilda). She began to cry and gave me a huge hug in mid-air 30,000 feet up! It just goes to show… anytime, anyplace, anyhow.

RELIEVING GUILT

Sometimes people can carry a lot of guilt regarding their loved ones. This was the case in a particular reading. A very sceptical man in his mid-60s had been ordered by his wife to have a reading with me. He sat across from me with his arms folded looking very stern. I suddenly picked up a brother figure and I knew he was only about 12 when he passed. He told me his brother, who was sitting in front of me, had always felt very responsible for his passing. I asked the young brother to show me the circumstances of his passing, and what I saw I relayed to this man, the whole sad event unfolding.

I saw the man drop his younger brother off at the football field and as the young man got out of the car, his brother gave him a paper bag with an apple and some sandwiches in it. For some reason the younger brother did not want to go to football that day, but the man made his brother go and dropped him off. I suddenly saw two planes collide in mid-air. Debris from the planes fell onto the football field and killed this man's younger brother.

This man had never forgiven himself for 50 years. He had taken so much guilt through his life, but his connection with his brother brought him so much peace that even many years of counselling could not bring. The man gave me a huge hug at the end of the reading as he knew with all the validation that I had been connecting to his family. They brought things through that only he knew. His wife sent me a huge bunch of flowers and told me, 'Thank you for giving me my husband back.' She then told me that for the first time in their 40 years together he had felt free of the guilt of his brother's passing.

READINGS FROM OBJECTS

It's not always people or animals that tell me things – sometimes it can be objects. This is called Psychometry. I may pick up an object and it can tell me a story, for example a personal item that has the person's energy in it. Such was the case of one lady who brought a ring to me. I generally do not need or want objects but she was quite insistent that I touch this object, and I immediately felt that it had belonged to a young lady who'd passed away because she was murdered. She was wearing the ring when she was murdered. The young lady and the ring told the lady having the reading the whole story surrounding this murder, some of which was then passed on to the police.

The police and the mother knew some of the details but the passed-over woman brought through more information. The police were then able to track down two other people involved in this drug-related murder of an innocent girl.

Another instance was when I went to a house in Maleny which a friend of mine had just moved into after buying it. I suddenly felt a presence of a female schoolteacher or principal. I also felt the house was telling me that it was two houses now joined together and that each house had come from different areas. My friend did some researching and found out that the house indeed was originally two houses. One of the houses had been a school from a local area, the second house was from Gympie, and many years before the two were joined, so my friend's investigation ended up proving that the feeling I was getting was right. There was nothing wrong with the joining of the houses as it was a good fit, but I just knew.

SEEING THINGS

Many of you will know the film, *The Sixth Sense,* and the moment when the young boy says that famous line, 'I see dead people.' Well, he's not the only one! One day I was driving in Sydney and I pulled up at a set of lights next to a hearse with a coffin in it. As I was side by side with this hearse, I saw an image of an elderly man sit up out of the coffin. He turned and looked at me and I could see him smiling, and he telepathically said to me, 'I'm Bert. I passed from cancer but I'm happy.' He then looked straight ahead and lay back down again. I sat there at the lights shaking my head slightly and having a bit of a laugh. He was such a sweet man! I then went home and went through the funeral notices and there was Bert being buried that day. At the ripe old age of 74, he had passed from cancer. When he'd looked at me, I could see he was probably in his mid-70s so everything he told me checked out.

Another incident was when I was conducting a face-to-face reading for a lady on the Gold Coast. She and I were facing each other when, to my left, I suddenly saw a very strong apparition of a black cat. The lady having the reading then also noticed the cat. We sat there watching this cat walk down beside the table. It went underneath my chair and we watched it come out from under my chair, walk away and just disappear. She and I looked at each other, quite amazed, and she said, 'You just saw that too, didn't you?' and I said, 'Yes, I did!' We both saw the image of her childhood cat called Sooty, who obviously wanted its presence known that day. These strange but true stories are just two of many that I could tell you about… and I might very well tell you more of them in another one of my upcoming books!

MY GUIDES

I've shared nearly everything I wanted to share with you in my first book detailing my amazing and very interesting life, but there's one group of beings I absolutely have to mention again – my Guides. I could absolutely not do what I do without my beautiful Guides. They have a great sense of humour and make me laugh often. Here are a couple of reasons why:

One year, we had just come to the end of the last reading for that year, when suddenly I saw my Guides putting on Hawaiian shirts with big straw hats and all running towards a plane with cameras around their necks and holding suitcases. They looked like they were all in a big hurry. I started to laugh as they were waving and running onto the tarmac and up the stairs into the plane. I then saw their little heads poking out the window waving at me. They showed me the front of the plane and it was like when there's a sign on the front of the bus with its destination – this one said 'Hawaii'. I could see them putting their suitcases up in the hand luggage compartment, waving to me and looking at me through the glass in the plane. I just had to laugh – they were going on holidays! It was like, 'We've worked hard, we're on holidays too.'

Another time I went to communicate and all I got was a sign of: 'Out to Lunch'. I laughed at that one! Then another time I was doing a late reading and when I went to connect to them I couldn't find them. I then saw them in this pub having a meal. I laughed again. So my Guides have a very, very good sense of humour!

CONCLUSION

I hope you've all enjoyed *My Journey Behind Blue Eyes* as much as I've enjoyed sharing it with you. I feel that I'm in a truly privileged position to be able to do what I do and to make such an impact on people's lives, and I hope you've now got some insight into what it means to be in my shoes. I'm also surrounded by my wonderful family – both living and passed over – who have supported me in my spiritual journey from the very beginning.

After I had my teachings from Ashkiya and my other Ascended Masters and Guides over that period of about 18 months that I've told you about, I doubted very much whether many had experienced what I had experienced, and my Guides confirmed that to me. I was one of only a handful on this planet meant to do what I was meant to do. It all became very clear to me about my life's work, which I'm now doing fulltime and absolutely loving.

During that time, I was shown that I would live to a ripe old age – into my 80s – and my last breath will probably be doing a reading for someone. What a great way to go! I was also shown that I will pass away quietly and peacefully in my own home after writing many books and doing many readings. And I have no fear of death.

So this is definitely not…

THE END.

Amanda's father, Edward (top photo); Amanda's mother, Jackie with her horse

GLOSSARY

Ascended Masters – highly evolved beings of pure love and intelligence. They are of a different realm from Spirit Guides.

Astral Travelling – when the soul decides to leave the body to travel to other realms or other physical places.

Body Talk – telepathically connecting to a person's body and allowing that body to express the physical problems going on within it.

Book of Akashik Records – records kept within the realms of the Guides and Ascended Masters of every person who has ever lived, is living now, and who lives in the future.

Medium – a person who acts as a channel to relay specific messages from loved ones passed over to loved ones still living.

Pranic Healing – corrects the energy imbalances that lie at the heart of illnesses and injuries. It uses up the negative energy and replaces it with the vital energy lifeforce called Prana.

Psychic – a person with the ability to connect to their Spirit Guides to bring through information for themselves or others.

Psychometry – sensing or reading the history of an object by touching it.

Spirit Guides – can be teachers, friends passed over, family passed over, pets passed over and loved ones passed over who guide us on our daily journey.

Spiritual Church – a place of worship for the practitioners of Spiritualism where the service is usually conducted by a medium.

Telepathic Communication – a type of communication that needs no physical words as it is imparted from spirit to mind.

Universal University – a university in a different realm from the physical realm where Amanda was taught how to be a medium by many teachers, Spirit Guides and Ascended Masters.

Wisdom Cards (specifically relating to the set mentioned in this book) – a set of cards with words of wisdom given to Amanda by many celebrities passed over.

Acknowledgements

Firstly, I'd like to thank everybody who has had anything to do with me making this book a reality. I am truly grateful, thankful and appreciative to the beautiful loved ones passed over – my Guides, my teachers, my Ascended Masters and my amazing celebrity Guides who have all helped me to bring this book to fruition.

I'd also like to thank my beautiful family for their support and love through this whole process.

I'd like to thank my many wonderful friends who have encouraged and helped me over the years to be who I am now. I value your constant input in helping me put this book together.

I'd also love to thank Louise Corran, my darling manager who is a source of constant strength to me on a daily basis, and my wonderful office staff, especially the lovely Rachel Langford. You are all amazing and I could not do this without you.

I'd like to thank Vicki Englund especially, for believing in me and the book and all the absolute hard work she has done to help me put this together. Thank you from the bottom of my heart.

As I told you at the beginning, my father, Edward, passed away as I was completing this book. Thank you, Dad, as you truly made this book possible. You are my strength. Forever in our hearts – Dad, Granddad and Great Granddad – loved so much by all of us. xxxxxxx

Writing This Book with Amanda

A few years ago, I interviewed Amanda De Warren on the phone for a story I was writing for *The Sunday Mail* newspaper in Brisbane. I wasn't particularly sceptical or a 'believer' but willing to see what I felt after our chat. Then right in the middle of the interview, Amanda had to interrupt us because both my recently passed-over mother and my father – who'd died when I was 12 – wanted to get messages to me. I was astounded by the relevance of those messages and know that there was absolutely no way Amanda could've known these things. It's that sort of story you hear over and over again and it's why I believe that Amanda De Warren is a genuine psychic, medium and animal communicator. I think this book will confirm that for many people, although Amanda's fans will obviously already know as they've experienced her gifts many times themselves.

I spent several months with Amanda either dictating her story to me as I typed madly away trying to keep up with her, or emailing me sections if she'd suddenly been inspired to add something new in between our meetings. The experiences described are astounding, from the numerous premonitions that came to fruition shortly after, to being able to see and speak to people passed-over even when she was a young child, to bringing through highly specific and very private information in her readings that she couldn't have known by any other means.

I've been amazed at some of the experiences Amanda has spoken about in the book. Admittedly, some of them sound way 'out there' but in the end it's really about the validation – people continually say that Amanda's insights into their private lives and histories and predictions about them are spot-on. I've certainly had a wonderful and fascinating time helping her to write the book – hearing about the passed-over famous people she's spoken with and received advice from, the teachings she received during her astral-travelling journeys, helping police solve crimes with her insights… and so much more.

At our final meeting for the book, I asked if Amanda would mind having a chat to my broody chook, Veronica, to try to get her to give up on being a mother. Amanda went down into my back yard, had the chat and said that the chook would probably be back to normal in about two days. (Anyone who's tried to change a broody hen's mind will know they go into a trance and don't want to be talked out of it.) Sure enough, exactly two days later Veronica was walking around as if she'd completely forgotten her previous obsession with staying on the nest. Australia's own 'animal whisperer' worked for me!

Amanda, thank you for a rewarding and enjoyable experience and for trusting me to help you tell your story.

Vicki Englund